Awaken

An Experiential Exploration of Enlightenment

DEAR DIVA,
GRACE ALWAYS!

LOVE
Sundar

SUNDAR KADAYAM

Poorna LLC
429 E Dupont Road #1041
Fort Wayne, Indiana 46825
http://poorna.one

Publisher's Cataloging-In-Publication Data

Names: Kadayam, Sundar, author.
Title: Awaken : an experiential exploration of enlightenment / Sundar
    Kadayam.
Description: [Fort Wayne, Indiana] : Poorna LLC, [2020] | Series: [The no-otherness series] |
    Include bibliographical references.
Identifiers: ISBN 9781734283501 (paperback) | ISBN 9781734283518 (hardback) | ISBN
    9781734283525 (ebook)
Subjects: LCSH: Kadayam, Sundar--Religion. | Enlightenment--Religious aspects--Hinduism. |
    Awareness--Religious aspects--Hinduism. | Self-consciousness (Awareness)--Religious
    aspects--Hinduism.
Classification: LCC BL1237.34 .K34 2020 (print) | LCC BL1237.34 (ebook) | DDC 294.5/4--dc23

Bhagavan Sri Ramana Maharshi

"Your own Self-realization is the greatest service you can render the world."

To the Light that shines forever

From that Light of Truth

This flow!

Praise

This is a masterful work. Wonderful...
A wonderful dialogue form that makes this rather difficult for the mind to absorb process easy in a step-by-step experiential process.
Wonderful!
In my humble opinion, it really works.

—Peter Cutler, monk, spiritual teacher, and author of *The Zen of Love*
https://n-lightenment.com/

If you want to be one with the holy fire in your heart, your innermost longing, but don't know how, read Awaken. You will be moved to the depth of your core, and when you finish the book, you will not be the same person anymore.

—Guthema Roba, mystic and author of Wake Up and Roar – *Poetry for meditation and awakening*
https://www.facebook.com/gbroba

What a gift this book from Sundar is. Every page you open you are rewarded with deep teachings, bringing us back to the sense of oneness. Sundar takes deep and ancient teachings of Advaita Vedanta and makes them accessible to us all in an easy-to-grasp, modern way. This book is for anyone who wants to find their authentic self.

—Jeff Emerson, yoga teacher, healer, and author of *Unfolding the Lotus*
https://www.truefreedomyoga.com/

Awaken is the book that will replace Khalil Gibran's The Prophet as the one book I will carry, if I was forced to pick just one book to take on a journey or vacation.

The concept of "Summa Iru" is something I am familiar with, having grown up in Tamil-speaking Chennai, India and as explained here alludes to the simplest and most practical Meditation and Spiritual Contemplation one can adopt.

Don't read this book; experience it. Blessings.

—Paul D'Souza, business strategist and mentor, author, healer, and spiritual teacher
http://www.pauldsouza.com/

Awaken quickly snaps you out of delusion into a "woke" state. Its simple narrative belies the deep wisdom it beholds. I had this incredible sense of peace soon after my first reading. It is more than a book. It is a like a pointer to the polestar. A reminder of who I am...

—Kanniks Kannikeswaran, PhD, composer and educator
http://kanniks.com/

Awaken is a gem among modern spiritual writings. A potent, relatable invitation to rest in the essential truth of oneself—the deep knowing, peace, and happiness that innately reside within each of us.

This gem has different facets, approaching the truth from more than one angle, with straightforward, step-by-step explanation on awakening; helpful guidance for returning to one's knowing after losing track of it in the vicissitudes of life;

and finally, profound, poetic utterances of wisdom that evoke inner reflection and stillness.

This is a clear, universal teaching to return to again and again!

—Max Raphael, healer and founder of True Resonance

https://www.trueresonance.net/

Awaken is an invitation to the heart of your true nature. It is a direct pointer to what is already present. Pure drops of nectar. Poetry for the heart of your being. The reader is invited to become the experience of who they are. This book is a shining light, a guide to awaken to the unchanging nature of the one, who is always present.

Gratitude for Sundar Kadayam. Thank you for your steadfastness and unwavering courage to stand in your true self and to shine the light upon the many paths for others to trace themselves.

—Maria Kammerer, healer and founder of Attune: The Art of Reiki

http://attunecincinnati.com

This is such a valuable piece of work that truly needs to be read and experienced by seekers all over the world! Sundar Kadayam offers many different simple and direct ways of finding the true self that the reader can experience in the moment. His heartfelt desire to help one wake up through awareness to realize the Pure Essence that is right here, right now, shines through his message and delivery. What a joy this book will bring to everyone who embraces it!!

—Sarah Dailey, healer and traditional Reiki teacher

This is excellent and a gift to the world that needs to be shared.

—Mark Hipskind, technologist and spiritual practitioner

Excellent. So clear.

—Patricia Diekman, healer and spiritual practitioner

The clear, step-by-step dialogue between teacher and student guides the reader to experience the truth of boundless awareness and then goes on to suggest ways to maintain that awareness of this essence in daily life. I would highly recommend this book to anyone interested in deepening their spiritual practice by entering silence and discovering their True Nature.

—Linda Hunnicutt Church, healer, spiritual practitioner, and traditional Reiki teacher

No matter where you are in your spiritual practice, this book will help you find a deeper stillness within. Through gentle prompts, we are guided to the truth that lies within each of us.

—Liz Nelson Wyan, human resources specialist and spiritual practitioner

I feel a deep truth and a clear understanding that speaks directly to my heart. At times it feels like to me how difficult it would be to try to explain and describe chocolate to someone who has never eaten chocolate. It was teaching from both sides, from the master and the student. I floated in the understanding throughout their conversation. Please don't ever stop writing and sharing this intimate dance with the holy self.

—Christine Hicks, healer and spiritual practitioner

Thank you for sharing a deep and soulful teaching. To experience the awareness of being aware is what I will hold close in my heart. A beautiful gift.

—Julie Anderson, healer, spiritual practitioner, and traditional Reiki teacher
http://www.otatararetreat.co.nz/

Awaken is a beautiful tool for understanding the Way. The dialogue between student and teacher creates stepping stones on the path of awareness—what a creative way to represent the process of discovery and understanding!

Thank you for sharing your perspective on the journey to Awaken.

—Denyce Peyton, healer, spiritual practitioner, traditional Reiki teacher, and researcher

What a delightful book! The Pointers are wonderful! Read the book once to get a sense of it, then read it very slowly again and again. This book is a daily devotional to read a bit at a time to fully absorb, integrate, and experience the Truth.

—Joyce Leonard, traditional Reiki teacher and practitioner
www.SantaCruzReikiWorks.com

Today the reading world received a great gift. Sundar's writings in Awaken are inspired from the Divine. He draws you in, as if you are the student, walking this path of enlightenment. You feel yourself embracing every word of the Master, following every step, every exercise, and experiencing the calm, serenity, and peace of deep meditations and "self." For me, Awaken replaces The Alchemist as my favorite read. Profound yet enriching and refreshing to the soul.

—Rev. Josanne K. Pagel, M.Div., MPAS,
PA-C, DFAAPA, Karuna® RMT

Awaken is a mindfully crafted book! There are layers of simplicity and depth. Whether you're a beginner or experienced in your quest of self-discovery and truth, there is plenty of substance for the soul. Definitely a book to cherish and refer back to! Thank you, Sundar, for a book from the heart!

—Deb Venable, Reiki practitioner,
clinical reflexologist, and holistic health consultant

Radiating with joy and Truth, this distillation of treasured wisdom is a gift of grace to the increasing number of practitioners holding space for a greater awakening.

—Julie Wheeler, healer, spiritual practitioner, and life and wellness coach

Awaken! Wonderfully written dialogue between a student and teacher, encouraging reflection and enlightenment. More than a great read, the dialogue encourages the reader to pause and contemplate the same form of questioning and introspection. Thanks for giving all of us in search an example of another and a guide to use in our daily practice.

—Doug Dennis, technologist, entrepreneur, and spiritual practitioner

This book is a brilliant blend of the wisdom of many religious teachings. I especially appreciate the prominent role the Reiki precepts play in your work. While I in all humility am not worthy to rank it among other great elucidations of the truth, I do wish to express that the processes you present constitute a continuing existential threat to my ego. Thank you. You have revealed dimensions to the projection of my delusion never before perceived. Like a sight that cannot be "unseen," these new perceptual techniques have accelerated my inevitable deep connection to all that is, to light speed. Well done!

—Joseph Moon, healer, spiritual practitioner, and nuclear scientist

An Invitation from the Heart

You can do many things to improve yourself!

But what are you going to do to know yourself?

After all, if you don't know who you really are

What is the point of all this stress you carry?

What is the point of all your fears and worries?

What is the point of all your judgments and anger?

What is the point of all your goals and achievements?

On whose behalf are you toiling in life like this?

The human form, with its creativity and intellect

Is a blessing to better explore life and living!

Why spend life exploring the outer world alone

When the greatest adventure lies in wait

For you to explore your own real nature?

The experiential knowing of your real nature

Is the beginning of the experience of deep peace

The real freedom that your heart yearns for!

This is an invitation for you to start this journey

This exhilarating adventure into
discovering the real You!

This is an experiential exploration of enlightenment!

Contents

Preface

May 4, 2015 was a strange day. I had a dizzy spell at lunch at home and was taken to the emergency center at the local hospital. That itself was unusual, because I rarely see a doctor and have had a hospital visit just once in my life when I was a young adult. What followed was something extraordinary. The six and a half hours of time spent in the hospital was one unbroken experience of peace, love, and gratitude. Even as I was poked with needles over and over and dragged around for various diagnostics, all there was, was this unbroken love for all. This was followed by a few days of incredible energy surges in the body that couldn't be contained.

I didn't always have "strange" experiences like this in my life.

In fact, I've had a career of thirty-three years as a commercial software developer, with twenty of those years as a technology entrepreneur. I've been a mix of the left-brained engineer, the rational skeptic, the problem solver, combined with the out-of-the-box thinker, visionary, dreamer, and "creative-idea" person.

I was also never a religious person, though I grew up in a household that practiced Hindu traditions and some rituals. However, I've always had a fond connection with Hanuman, the Hindu deity, from the time I was a child.

I moved to the USA in 1988 and have been living in Cincinnati, Ohio through summer of 2019. I've had a strong career, with growing levels of opportunities and successes, while leading a conventional suburban life with my wife and two children.

It was in August 2000, that the direction of my life changed. My father was struck down with a series of strokes than left him in a coma, paralyzed from neck down. The man who was given up for being practically dead, miraculously returned home to live out another three years. However, those extra three years were so laced with pain and suffering that it pushed me into exploring ways to help him, which took me to this healing system called Reiki. This thrust me into a whole new world of healing, miracles, and spiritual awakening.

Since 2001, I did healing work for hundreds of people and in turn have been a witness to the reality of healing miracles that occur right in our midst, but was previously completely unaware of. In 2007, I met Frans Stiene, who has been a foremost teacher of the traditional system of Reiki, which was not just a healing system, but a path to Self-realization. With his guidance, I took my own practice seriously and have steadily experienced shifts in reality that are difficult to rationally explain. Many noteworthy spiritual experiences have happened that I can only label as "miracles."

Later in 2013, events led me to the teachings of Papaji and then to his teacher, Sri Ramana Maharshi. This was followed by connections to contemporary nondual teachers like Rupert Spira, Mooji, Sri Nochur Venkataraman, and Peter Cutler.

At one level, the strange events of May 4, 2015 can be seen as a continuation in this unlikely journey of an engineer deep into spirituality. But what happened on that day and the days that followed was notably different. The fireworks of extraordinary spiritual experiences that I'd witnessed before were set aside, and a simple peace-love started becoming a foundation, all on its own.

Onward to June 7, 2016. I was sitting at a Cincinnati airport gate, waiting to board a Frontier flight to San Francisco. There was about thirty-five minutes left to board the flight, when this intuition, this heart-whisper, emerged. "It is time to write." One beautiful blessing of my spiritual practice has been this ability to distinguish between a heart-whisper and a plain thought, and the sheer courage and determination to follow the intuition without questioning. I did so at this time, opening up my laptop to an empty Word document. I paused. Then the flow began. I typed as fast as I could, boarded the flight, and reopened the laptop when I could. I continued typing as the blessed flow continued. All through the bumpy, tightly squeezed flight to San Francisco, on the bus with wings that was the Frontier flight, the flow flowed, and the typing followed. Five minutes before landing, the flow stopped.

When I got to my hotel and reopened the Word document, reading for the first time what had flowed, I realized that there is something of value to share with the world. This is the first section you see in this work, above, "Exploration," the dialogue between the Master and the Student, enabling an experiential exploration of Reality, a direct glimpse of enlightenment!

I sent out a first draft with just the "Exploration" to fellow practitioners, friends, and others in 2016. Peter Cutler was among this first set of people who read this and affirmed the value of the pointers it contained. After that, I let the work marinate, because it didn't feel ready for a broader offering.

Since then, a few more experiences have facilitated a deepening of wakefulness.

In June 2017, I sat in a talk by Sri V. Ganesan in Ramanashramam, the ashram of the great awakened sage, Sri Ramana Maharshi, in Tiruvannamalai, India. He is the grandnephew of Sri Ramana Maharshi. He grew up in the company of many of the people who awakened around the great sage! After the talk, I approached him, in tears, to express my gratitude for his clear pointers to Reality. He touched my heart center and said, "The real guru, Bhagavan, the Sadhguru, is right here inside you!" And something shifted deeply that over time has remained as a steady, aware presence. What a blessing!

In July 2018, I participated in a seven-day Satsang with Sri Nochur Venkataraman in Chennai, India. This entire experience caused a deepening of awareness. But one specific exchange with the Master was so important to my journey. I asked him, "Why am I feeling this painful oscillation between Reality and the unreal?" and he said, "What is oscillating will oscillate until it won't!" For a while, that didn't make much sense to me, but I still took it as a pointer to be patient. And as life unfolded from there, an experiential steadiness of awareness dawned, regardless of the content of experiences. In effect, the oscillation slowed down a lot as the Master pointed.

In October 2018, Frans Stiene came back to Cincinnati for a surprise visit and stayed with me. One night, sitting across the dinner table, as I was sharing the state of the journey, Frans felt a movement within him to offer a spiritual blessing, and I was so ready to receive the same. What followed was an experience in which the last vestige of the belief in a separate identity fell away. What was left was just an expansive presence that could not be contained in the body. Presence shone within and without, and as all things.

Now, in 2019, as I write this, the time seemed right to share this work. It felt more authentic to put this together in a form that could be shared more broadly, because the oscillation between ego-self and true self has lessened considerably now.

I share all this is, not to say that "I am special." Quite the opposite. It is to shine the mirror of Truth in front of you to say, "You are special." Wake up to recognize who you are, and be free!

This work is now presented to you as a heart offering.

May the blessings that awakened the Masters be with you too!

Introduction

Something in your heart recognizes this invitation to explore your real nature. Thank you for picking up this work.

Whether you are a sincere spiritual practitioner waiting to experience real freedom, or you are interested in exploring life deeply, or you are just curious about what enlightenment is, to you, the seeker—this work is offered.

As you navigate life, you've had goals and achievements, losses and failures, regrets and resentments, love and judgments, anger and fear, and maybe some gratitude and generosity. Through it all, you know—somewhere deep within you—that there is more to life than meets the eye. You have a yearning to know how to be free from these ups and downs. You have an inner desire to be free, really free.

But who is this person you think you are? What is the nature of this "I" for whom you are doing all this? Have you ever paused to explore who is this "I" you think of yourself to be?

Before the believer and the nonbeliever

Before beliefs and the lack of beliefs

Before believing and not believing

Lies the field of Being!

Religions want you to believe

Spirituality wants you to Be

Reality is already this Being

You are that Reality!

Behind the veil of your own self-image lies the Truth of who you really are! The experiential recognition of this Truth is pure freedom. Freedom from the limitations of your perceived self-image. Freedom from the ups and downs that accompany the experience of life as a separate person.

This experiential recognition of Truth has been called by various names, such as Enlightenment, Awakening, Self-realization, and so on.

The character in this work is a young, ardent seeker who sits with his Master to explore Reality. What unfolds is an experiential exploration of Reality and Awakening, as the Awakened Master leads his young student into the direct experience of Truth.

If you were attracted to this work, you probably have spent a lot of time seeking knowledge, steadily improving yourself, or maybe following a committed spiritual path. . . and yet something seems to be missing! Even if you have had transcendental experiences, Truth may seem just out of reach, and you may be disappointed. Perhaps you've practiced for decades and find that the big breakthrough you've been waiting to experience is ever so near, but still so far. Perhaps you've been trying to get rid of your ego, and that has not been working out well, and you yearn for something that will set you free. For you, I offer this work.

Unlike traditional books, this work is an invitation for your direct experience. The reason is this: you cannot gain knowledge that will lead to knowledge of this Reality. Direct experience alone can precipitate the realization of your real nature.

As a result, here are some ways you can approach this work.

1. **Experience it directly right away.** If you feel open to following the guidance, without necessarily having to know what it is and where it is taking you, please follow the "Exploration" section experientially. Put yourself in the shoes of the student. Experience the questions being posed as your own. Listen keenly to the Master's suggestions and questions. As they unfold, experience the student's answers and feelings as your own. Pause as the student pauses to let the experience fully arise.

2. **Read it once, and experience it a second time.** If you feel like you'd do better if you knew the lay of the land and where you are being guided, then read this work once. Then come back a second time to experience the work, following the approach above.

What follows is not created afresh. Great Masters from various ages have talked about a direct experiential knowing of Reality, of Truth. Their conversations with their students, their guidance to the seeker, and their Light have flowed in these words.

All errors in what follows are due to flaws in this instrument and not with the Great Masters and the Flow of What Is.

Part 1 - Exploration

The student, a young and ardent seeker, visits the Master, with a question about the nature of Reality. What ensues is a guided, experiential exploration of Reality and Enlightenment.

The Direct Experience

Student: Master, please tell me about the nature of reality.

Master: *[sets out a set of five gold ornaments]* See this. Here's a ring, bracelet, necklace, earrings, and a nose ring. How do they appear to you?

Student: I see a ring, a bracelet, a necklace, a pair of earrings, and a nose ring.

Master: So, they appear to you as different objects?

Student: Yes, that is how I see them.

Master: But each of these is made from gold. Is the ring separate from the gold from which it is made? Is the bracelet separate from the gold it is made of?

Student: No, Master. They are all gold.

Master: So, these five different objects are all gold and are inseparable from the gold of which they are made. Is that right?

Student: Yes.

Master: If I somehow took the gold away from these objects, would any of these objects exist?

Student: No. There would be no ring without the gold. No bracelet without the gold.

Master: These different objects have a common underlying reality, which is gold. Is that right?

Student: Yes.

Master: Even as you now see the five different objects, you can also see that they are the made of same essence—gold. Is that true?

Student: Yes. I can now see it clearly.

Master: Reality is like this. You and I and this table and that window and the tree out there—all these look like different objects. But in fact, they have the same underlying essence.

Student: Master, I can see the analogy quite clearly. But I appear to be so different from you and so different from the tree. What underlying essence could be the same for me and you and that tree?

Master: This essence is present everywhere and at any time. It is the underlying essence of all things. In this sense, it is infinite and it is eternal. There never has been and never will be a thing not made of this essence. This effectively boggles the mind. Because of the underlying essence of things, the mind cannot put this essence into a neat, conceptual box. Despite the fact that the mind cannot conceptualize this essence, this essence does exist.

Student: If the mind can't conceptualize this essence, how has anyone known of this essence?

Master: When the mind is laid to rest, in silence, the essence can be experienced. Except this experience cannot be conceptualized as this or that.

Student: Is this essence God? Is this essence the Holy Spirit? Is this essence some kind of quantum field?

Master: God, Holy Spirit, quantum field—these are conceptual labels meant to describe conceptual ideas. The essence cannot be labeled, and what can be labeled is not this essence.

Student: In that case, can you tell me what the experience of this essence feels like?

Master: This essence is aware without concepts. It feels like peace that is unbroken. It feels like love without its opposite. As such, it feels like a kind of happiness, a bliss that cannot be described by the mind.

Student: That sounds beautiful. How can I experience this essence?

Master: You, the real you, are this essence. Just like I, my real self, am this essence. This essence is already present here and now, like the gold in the ring or the bracelet. What obscures this essence is your sense that you are separate from it. It is as if the ring somehow feels separate and different from the gold that is its essence.

Student: If this essence is my real nature, like gold is the real nature of the ring or the bracelet, what is this sense of me being a distinct, a separate individual person, different from all people and things around me? I do see myself as a unique individual. And yet you tell me that this sense of me feeling like a unique individual is what is keeping me from seeing the essence, which is who I truly am! I'm confused!

Master: When you are out on a sunny day and wear black sunglasses, how does the world appear to you? Does it still appear to you like the world that is vivid and bright?

Student: No. When I wear black sunglasses, the world appears to be dim. That is what the sunglasses do, so the brightness of the sun and its reflection on the surrounding structures do not hurt my eyes.

Master: So, when you wear black sunglasses, the world appears different, less bright than it actually is. Colors don't quite look the same, right?

Student: Yes, that is right.

Master: Now, what happens if instead of black sunglasses, you wore sunglasses with a distinct blue tint? Does the world look different?

Student: Yes. Everything I see will have a blue tint while being less bright.

Master: OK. Let's say that your eyesight is normal and that you don't need prescription glasses. What would happen if you wore prescription glasses meant for people with nearsightedness? Would the world look different?

Student: Yes, Master. Everything would look distorted to me. Nothing would appear as it normally does to me.

Master: Now, instead of prescription glasses, let's say I gave you the glass carved out of the bottom of a soda bottle, and I asked you to look through it instead. What would the world look like?

Student: I think everything would look very distorted. I think that is because the bottle glass has a lot of uneven thickness. And looking through it, I might not even recognize things well.

Master: Yes, the world would look seriously distorted indeed. You see, all these different forms of lenses and glasses create different distortions and affect the way you see the world. Looking at the world through our minds is just like this. What the eyes register as light reflections, the mind interprets as a world full of people, objects, and places. There is the world, and then there is our intellectual, conceptual model of it, full of "trees," "lakes," "the sky," "people," "animals," "birds," and things like these. Seeing and interacting with the world through this conceptual model makes it impossible to see the essence underlying all these apparently different things.

Student: Master, I see what you are saying. This mind distorts my ability to see the world as it is. This mind is what is hiding from me the true essence of who I really am. But how can I exist without having my mind interpret what the senses of sight, taste, sound, touch, and smell tell me? How could I even exist in this world without my mind interpreting it?

Master: That is a good question. But before we delve into that, notice that the mind is not just interpreting and conceptualizing the world of things around you. It is also doing it on behalf of who you think you are, this person with an identity, with a personality, with experiences, memories, desires, attachments, emotions, and such. It is doing this on behalf of a person with a self-image. Correct?

Student: Yes, Master. That is true. I am Carter. I am a twenty-four-year-old Caucasian male. I am a graduate in physics. I am keenly interested in the structure of our world, the very structure of our reality. I am a lover of music and movies. I am an explorer. I am a learner, and I am also a seeker of truth. Yes, this is my sense of who I am. And I definitely do see the world from this lens of my self-image.

Master: You can then see that your mind works on behalf of this identity you have, and in turn, it interprets what it encounters in the world based on your beliefs, your likes and dislikes, your fears and worries, and so forth. Is this right?

Student: Yes, Master. When I see a person, I observe what they are wearing and how they walk and talk. In turn, I am forming opinions and judgments about that person. Maybe I will label them as "obese," or "rude," or "stupid," or "smart," or whatever. And now I can see that once I label them, all I am doing is interacting with this internal image I have made of that person and not who they are. Would they truly deserve the judgments and labels I apply to them? Would those labels be the objective truth or my own opinion only? I understand, Master. I can see how the mind distorts my view of the world itself.

Master: As a seeker of truth, you are indeed open to the exploration, and this is good.

Student: Thank you, Master. Does this all mean that I need to change my mind? That I need to look into my personality and find where I'm wrong in my beliefs and change that?

Master: Changing your mind, changing your beliefs, changing your personality—these things can have some practical benefits. But all you would be doing is changing one set of beliefs with something else, one set of likes and dislikes with something else. This is self-improvement, and it has some limited value. More importantly, all this is based on the foundational assumption that you are indeed a separate person with a separate and distinct identity, right?

Student: Yes, I see that. Underlying all this is the sense that I am this, and I am that. And that sense is extremely real.

Master: Indeed. That sense of "I am" does seem very real. But who is this "I am"? Have you ever explored this to find the truth of who you think you are?

Student: No, Master. I have always assumed this sense of "I am"—that "I am Carter," that "I am a twenty-four-year-old Caucasian male."

Master: Nearly all people in the world are like this. We reach out into the outer world to seek grand explorations and adventures. And yet, we miss the greatest exploration, the most profound adventure of all, which is to know who you really are!

Student: I agree, Master. How do I begin this exploration?

Master: It is easily done, here and now, if you are ready.

Student: Yes, Master. I'm ready to do this. I want to explore the truth of who I am. I want to experience the

23

essence that you speak of, the essence of which I'm made, just as you are.

Master: There is one thing you have to do as we proceed on this exploration. You must set aside your mind in answering my questions. What I mean is that I need you to answer from your current experience, in the moment, and not from what you know as "knowledge" in your mind. I'll help you with this too.

Student: I understand, Master. You've already explained well that it is the mind running on behalf of my sense of being "Carter." This mind is what is keeping me from experiencing my essence. I understand why you are asking to set this mind aside in answering your questions. I'll do this.

Master: OK. Take a deep breath, and relax yourself physically. For the next few minutes, you don't need to engage with your mind's anxious pursuits. You can simply remain present here in this exploration with me.

Student: [*breathes deeply and relaxes*]

Master: Look out the window at the tree.

Student: [*turns attention to the tree*]

Master: What are you seeing?

Student: A tree.

Master: How do you know you are seeing the tree?

Student: I think my mind interpreted what my eye saw, and from memory I knew it is a tree. That is how I knew that I was seeing a tree.

Master: You had to reach into your mind's memory to know this was a tree. But that is OK. It's good that you were aware of this. Now tell me, how did you know that your mind interpreted what the eyes saw as a "tree"?

Student: [*pauses*] I've never thought to ask this before. How did I know that my mind knew this was a tree? Wow! Let me pause a bit here. [*pauses and appears to ponder*] I think I noticed a thought that said, "It is a tree."

Master: And how did you know that there was a thought?

Student: [*pauses*] Was it another thought through which I knew the first thought? No, that can't be.

Thoughts don't know of other thoughts, because I've already noticed that thoughts come in a sequence in my mind. And yet there is *something* that seems to know, that seems to be aware of my thinking and the stream of thoughts, especially when I'm not lost in them.

Master: Yes, there is something that seems to be aware of thoughts. Thoughts come and go. We can say that thoughts rise and fall. Can you simply remain as a witness of your thoughts? Can you simply notice the rising and falling of thoughts? Just for a little while. Now.

Student: [*goes quiet and gently closes his eyes, remaining quiet for a minute or so*]

Master: What was the nature of your experience in this past minute?

Student: A thought arose, and I noticed it rising and falling. Another one followed, and I was aware of it rising and falling. And so on. But this is the first time I've noticed so keenly the coming and going of these thoughts. It seemed like everything was happening in slow motion. Thoughts didn't seem to rush one after the other as they usually do in my normal experience. Instead, thoughts seemed to rise and fall slowly, to be followed by another one a little bit later, doing the same.

Master: Yes. When you start noticing thoughts as a witness, and don't engage in the thinking, or get lost in the thinking, it all seems to slow down. But through this minute, you were aware of the thoughts coming and going, right?

Student: Yes.

Master: So, you've now experienced awareness of thoughts coming and going. Right?

Student: Yes.

Master: There is an *awareness* that seems to *be aware* of the thoughts. Right?

Student: Yes.

Master: So the eyes registered the light, and the mind interpreted it as a tree. The thought "It is a tree" arose, and you were aware of that thought. If you were not aware of the thought, "It is a tree," would you have known about the tree?

Student: [*pauses*] No. If I were not aware of the thought, I would not have known of the thought, and in turn, I would not have known the content of the thought: "It is a tree."

Master: Yes. Without awareness, can thoughts be known?

Student: No.

Master: And without thoughts, a world of objects cannot be known, right?

Student: That's right.

Master: So it would be right to say that without awareness, the world of objects cannot be known, right?

Student: That's right.

Master: Or, put another way, it is through awareness that thoughts and the world of objects are known, right?

Student: That's right. Being aware of thoughts makes the thoughts known, and the world of objects that the thoughts conceptually describe are known.

Master: It is through awareness that all things are known.

Student: Indeed.

Master: Now look at the tree again. What is your experience of seeing it?

Student: [*looks at tree*] My eyes are seeing it. The thought "It is a tree" arises. And I am aware of that thought. And that is how I know that I am seeing a tree.

Master: Is this your current experience? Or are you citing this from memory?

Student: This is my current experience. I am aware of the thought "It is a tree," and I am also aware of the seeing of the tree.

Master: Since it is through awareness that this tree was known, and as all things are known, what knows that you are aware?

Student: [*pauses... some time passes in silence*] itself? Awareness is what knows of itself? Awareness is what is aware that I am aware.

Master: Now close your eyes. Notice your thoughts and body sensations.

Student: [*closes eyes and follows the guidance*]

Master: Now notice your awareness of being aware.

Student: [*silence ensues... a couple of minutes pass*]

Master: Now gently open your eyes. What is your experience of being aware of being aware?

Student: Silence. A sense of emptiness—as in no thoughts, no objects.

Master: Was the sense of emptiness truly empty? Was nothing, no thing, present?

Student: There was nothing present.

Master: How did you know there was nothing present?

Student: I was aware of it! [*pauses and then laughs*] I was aware of it. Awareness was present.

Master: Did you experience anything else?

Student: It felt peaceful like I've never experienced being peaceful.

Master: Was anything lacking or missing when you were experiencing this?

Student: No. I felt content.

Master: This is the experience of your essence, the experience of your true nature. It is simply awareness— awareness that is self-aware and simply present. The experience feels like unbroken peace. The feeling of contentment is happiness without its opposite. This is the experience of who you truly are.

Student: [*closes eyes and takes a deep breath, then minutes pass*]

Master: Beyond the filtering lens of your mind, beyond the veils that thinking introduces, lies your true essence. And you now have an experiential knowledge of yourself as that awareness, the essence of who you truly are.

Student: [*opens eyes and gazes at the Master, as a couple of minutes pass*]

Master: This essence is not just your essence. It is mine too. And that of the tree, this window, the room, the table, and everything and everyone. This essence was the essence of all things yesterday, the last year, a million years ago. This essence is the essence that will remain the essence tomorrow, ten years from now, a million years from now. This essence is not just the essence of you, me, and the objects in the world around you and me. It is the essence of everything in the remote village in Africa, in the depths of the Pacific ocean, in the busy streets of China, in the theater in India, in the moon, in the planets, in the Sun, in faraway galaxies, and in all of creation. This essence is thus infinite, ever present.

Student: [*remains silent*]

Master: Don't take my word for it. Make sure this is your experience. Close your eyes. Become aware of your thoughts and sensations. Be aware of being aware.

Student: [*closes eyes as a minute passes*]

Master: Notice if the awareness is contained in just your body or if it can be noticed outside your body—

above it, behind it, below it. . . Let me know where its edge is, beyond which there is no awareness.

Student: [*silence continues*] I can't find a boundary to the awareness. It is everywhere.

Master: Now, recollect with your mind the situation in which you were this morning at 9 a.m. Vividly recall that situation in your mind with as much detail as you can muster. Let me know when you are there.

Student: [*pauses*] I am there.

Master: As yourself at 9 a.m. today, now become aware of your thoughts, sensations, and the world of objects around you. And then be aware of being aware.

Student: [*pauses*] I am aware of being aware.

Master: Notice if there is any boundary to the awareness.

Student: [*pauses*] I can't find a boundary to the awareness. It is everywhere.

Master: Now, vividly recollect a scene or situation from your childhood. Let me know when you are there.

Student: [*pauses*] I am there. It is a wonderful time when I got great gifts at my tenth birthday party.

Master: As yourself, the ten-year-old, now become aware of your thoughts, sensations, and the world of objects and people around you. Then be aware of being aware.

Student: [*pauses*] I am aware of being aware.

Master: Notice if there is any boundary to the awareness.

Student: [*pauses*] No, I can't find a boundary to the awareness. It is everywhere.

Master: Now, picture what you were planning to do at 9 a.m. tomorrow. Let me know when you are there.

Student: [*pauses*] I am in a meeting with my team at work.

Master: As yourself tomorrow morning, become aware of your thoughts, sensations, and the world of objects and people around you. Then be aware of being aware.

Student: [*pauses*] I am there.

Master: Notice if there is any boundary to the awareness.

Student: [*pauses*] No. I can't find a boundary to the awareness. It is everywhere.

Master: Go ahead and gently open your eyes. Is the essence of who you really are—this awareness that is aware of itself—unbounded by space and unchanging across time?

Student: Yes, Master. That is my experience. This awareness is infinite, unbounded. It is also the very same no matter when in time I notice it. Indeed, it is infinite, and it is unchanging in time.

Master: Are you experiencing your specific essence, or are you experiencing the essence that underlies everything, every one, and all experiences?

Student: The latter, Master. I am experiencing *the* essence that underlies everything, every one, and all experiences.

Master: Now who is experiencing *the* essence of it all?

Student: I am.

Master: Let us look at this "I am" and the "I" underlying it. Is that "I" experiencing *the* essence of it all, the one known as "Carter"?

Student: [*pauses*] I am not sure. This "I" does feel like "Carter," but I am not sure.

Master: OK. Where do you think this "I" is present?

Student: I think this "I" called "Carter" is present in my body.

Master: Let us systematically look at where this "I" is. Go ahead and close your eyes. Is this "I" in the lower half of your body, below your torso?

Student: [*pauses*] Yes, I think this "I" is there in the lower part of the body.

Master: Imagine that through an accident, the lower part of your body had to be cut off. Would this "I" be gone, disappeared, or in some way diminished? Experience this now and tell.

Student: No, Master. The sense of this "I" is still there.

Master: So this "I" must be in the upper part of your body, then? Is it in the chest, below the neck?

Student: I think this "I" may be in the chest.

Master: Imagine that through another accident, all that could be saved is the upper part of the body, above the neck. With the body below the neck gone, has the "I" disappeared? Experience this now and tell.

Student: No, Master. The sense of this "I" is still there.

Master: So this "I" must be in your head. Let us divide the head into four parts: upper left, upper right, lower left, and lower right. And imagine that for some serious reason, we had to cut away each of these sections, starting with the lower right. Is the "I" gone?

Student: No. Still there.

Master: Lower left is now gone. Is the "I" gone?

Student: No. Still there.

Master: Upper right is now gone. Is the "I" gone?

Student: No. Still there.

Master: Upper left is now gone. Is the "I" gone?

Student: No. Still there.

Master: Well. There is no body now, and is your experience that there is still an "I"?

Student: Yes, the sense of "I" is still there.

Master: With no body, no brain, there should be no mind. So, what you are saying is that in your experience now, without a body and mind, there is still the sense of an "I." Is that right?

Student: Yes, the sense of "I" is still there.

Master: With no body and mind to house the "I," where might this "I" be?

Student: [*pauses*] Everywhere!

Master: [*remains in silence*]

Student: [*pauses*] The "I" is everywhere. [*laughs and opens eyes*] Wow! Like awareness, which was everywhere and unchanging in time, this "I" is everywhere, too.

Master: [*remains silent*]

Student: Awareness alone is present as the essence, everywhere, all the time. This "I" must be the "I" of awareness.

Master: [*continues to remain in silence*]

Student: The "I am" I've felt all along is the "I am" of the essence, the "I am" of my true nature, the "I am" of awareness.

Master: [*continues to remain in silence*]

Student: There is no separate "I" called "Carter." It categorically could not be found. Yet, the "I" and the "I am" that continued to be present was that of awareness.

Master: [*still silent*]

Student: If there is no separate "I" in here called "Carter," there is no separate "I" in there called "Master," no separate "I" in anyone.

Master: [*still silent*]

Student: [*laughs*] Holy shit! There's never been a separate "I" anywhere. Just the pure essence that is awareness!

Master: [*smiles*]

Student: Awareness, in the guise of apparent bodies and minds, experiences an infinitely colorful and diverse world of separate objects. Every now and then, in a given body and mind, awareness comes to a resolution of knowing itself as awareness. Is that what happened here, Master?

Master: [*smiles*] Yes, dear one. In that body and mind given the label "Carter," awareness realized itself as awareness.

Student: [*exults*] This is what the sages have called enlightenment, right?

Master: [*smiles*] Yes. This has been called by many labels. Enlightenment. Nirvana. Moksha. Awakening. Self-realization. But those are just labels for the experience of awareness realizing itself. This "enlightenment" isn't something you as a separate identity called "Carter" achieved. So "enlightenment" isn't an achievement, as it has been mistaken by many. "So-and-so achieved enlightenment" we say loosely, but there is no "so-and-so" to achieve anything. After all, your experience vividly showed the absence of a separate identity called "Carter," did it not?

Student: [*smiles and nods*]

Master: This occurrence, this experience of awareness realizing itself as awareness through an apparently separate body and mind, is seen as freedom. The ultimate freedom. Can you see why?

Student: Yes, Master. There is no separate "I" to experience any limitation anymore. Freedom is the recognition of and being the infinite and eternal awareness. All bondage, limitation, suffering, and issues were that of "Carter's." "Carter" does not exist. Awareness alone is. This is why this experience is deemed the ultimate freedom.

Master: Yes, dear one, that is right.

Student: [*pauses and contemplates*] Will this body-mind [*points to self*] be permanently free of "Carter," or will "Carter" rise again through the force of habit of my twenty-four years of living as "Carter"?

Master: This is a brilliant question. "Carter" does not exist. But this body-mind contains echoes and impressions of having lived as a "Carter." Your liking for sweets, your liking for outdoor exploration, your liking of new experiences, your dislike of dogma, your dislike of judgmental people...all these are impressed upon the body-mind, like footsteps left behind on sand when one walks the beach over and over. You may encounter a pull to indulge in sweets, say, and that might appear to be as if "Carter" has returned to control the body-mind. But that is not true. A separate identity called "Carter" does not exist. An echo or impression might arise of what appears to be "Carter," but you can always do this inner exploration that we did, to see if there is a separate "I" called "Carter." Every single time, it will lead to the same experiential conclusion that there is no separate "I" called "Carter."

Student: I feel an immense clarity in the body and an immense peace in the mind. I feel viscerally different than I did when we started talking. Going into the world, leaving your graceful presence, will I continue to feel this way?

Master: There is a permanent shift that has occurred just now. You have experientially glimpsed the truth of your essence, of the very essence of it all. Yet you will encounter your family members, friends, coworkers, and other people, just like you have experienced before. And the body-mind may react from its old patterns. You might get angry or feel fear. But there will be one difference. You can always explore who is feeling all this and return quickly to the essence of it all: awareness. By remaining in the state of being aware of being aware, you can remain in and as the essence. And the more you do this, as a practice in abiding as awareness, the less and less the body-mind will feel the past pulls of reactions, judgments, anger, and worries. More and more the body-mind will experience the unbroken peace of awareness, and it will permeate through all experiences.

Student: Master, is this why, in the presence of realized masters, one can feel the peace automatically?

Master: What distinguishes a body-mind of a realized Master, your body-mind now, and that of others in the world is this: the so-called realized Master abides in and as the essence of awareness at all times in all places. You, after this experience, will notice that this body-mind is sometimes stabilized and experiences awareness alone and at other times is caught in the drama of the world. Others, who have not undertaken this sort of inner exploration, will more or less experience the drama of the world alone in their body-minds. The body-mind of a realized Master who abides in awareness and as awareness behaves like a tuning fork, causing the body-mind of those who approach the Master to resonate, bringing forth their essence of pure awareness to the foreground of experience. This is why peace is experienced in the presence of a realized Master.

Student: Master, we have heard stories of people who, after the awakening experience, automatically transform into the state of abidance in and as the essence of awareness. These people are totally free and are not affected by their past lives as separate identities, and they are free to simply be present as the essence of awareness at all times. How does this occur?

Master: You can readily see that the world of objects is diverse. There are so many different circumstances into which a person can be born and raised, and infinite are the experiences across different people at different eras of this world. To that extent, even the phenomenon of awareness realizing itself in a body-mind happens in a variety of ways. In some rare people, there is indeed a spontaneous realization and clearance of the body-mind, of the artifacts and echoes of a separate identity. In the vast majority of cases where Self-realization has occurred, a time period may elapse before the body-mind is cleared of the echoes of the separate "I."

Student: So awakening could be separated in time from total clearance of the body-mind! Awakening and abidance need not occur together.

Master: Yes.

Student: In this case, with this body-mind [*gestures to self*], there could be times in the day where I can remain aware of being aware, remain in the true essence, and there could be other times when I am lost in the drama. Could this happen?

Master. Yes. And it occurs often in most people. That is why it is wise to undertake a practice of abidance in the essence of awareness, a practice that, in time, can clear out the body-mind of all remaining echoes of the past times spent as "Carter."

Student: What is this practice that is suitable for me?

Master: A core practice is Self-Inquiry. When you feel caught in the drama and react to life as a separate "I"—if you notice "Carter" lashing out at the world or feeling anxious—you can know that you have slipped away from the state of being pure awareness. When you notice this, simply inquire "Who is feeling this way?" And just as we did here together, follow the trail from the feeling to that which knows of it and knows itself: awareness. When you arrive at awareness, simply remain aware of being aware for as much time as you can.

Student: Yes, Master. This makes sense. But should I proactively incorporate a practice that will let me not slip back into the drama of "Carter"?

Master: Yes, you can. This very same practice of being aware of being aware you can do in a more regular manner without needing a world trigger to cause you to get there. You could incorporate, say, five minutes, ten minutes, or even an hour of simply sitting in a comfortable place, to the place of being aware. Then simply rest in the awareness of being aware.

Student: That sounds good. Are there other techniques or practices that can help with the deepening of abidance in the essence of awareness?

Master: One of my favorite techniques is "resting in the heart." Find a quiet place and at least five minutes of time for yourself (more is better, but at least five minutes are necessary). Ensure that you will not be disturbed by calls, notifications, or whatever other distractions may arise. Close your eyes. Take a deep breath down into your belly, and physically relax yourself. Take another deep breath, and take that physical relaxation even deeper. Take one more deep breath to deepen that relaxation. Now, gently move your attention from your head (where it is probably feeding a stream of thoughts), down into your heart center. The heart center is located between the two rib cages, to the right of the physical heart. It's also known as the "heart chakra" in some traditions. Let your attention rest in the heart center. With your attention resting in the heart center, notice if there is any attention that is feeding the mind, body sensations, or external stimuli, such as noise in the room. If so, gently withdraw that attention down into the heart center. With all the attention in your heart center, now let the attention drop, falling into the depths of the heart center. Attention is like a wave rising from the ocean of awareness. Deep in your heart center, this ocean of awareness is palpably experienced. Let the wave of attention drop into the ocean of awareness in your heart center. And let the wave of attention dissolve into the ocean of awareness. Awareness alone is present now. Rest in that awareness. Be that silence of that awareness. Nothing to do. No thoughts to pursue. No pull to process the stimuli of the outer world. Just the ocean of awareness. Rest here for a while, at least five minutes. When you are ready to return to the world of objects and things and people, allow that awareness to rise as attention into your heart center, and let it gently feed and engage the body-mind. Let that peace of resting in the heart permeate your world of activity. Let that silence nurture your every waking moment in the world.

Student: This is delectable. I am going to love this technique of "resting in the heart." Are there any other techniques I should be aware of to navigate the world without losing my anchoring in awareness? Are there any techniques that will proactively help clear this body-mind of past impressions and echoes of "Carter"?

Master: Yes, there are plenty of other techniques one could practice. When you engage the world of objects, it will help to remember and practice these precepts:

Just for today
Do not bear anger
Do not worry
Be grateful
Be true to your way and being
Be compassionate to yourself and others

Student: This makes sense to me, Master. When engaging the world of objects without anger or judgment, without worry or fear, with gratitude in my heart, being true to myself and being compassionate to myself and others, all these seem like they would return me to the state of pure essence—awareness. Is that right?

Master: Yes, living in the moment, in accordance with these precepts, is a way to keep returning to pure essence that is awareness. Of these, the practice of gratitude is the master key. It is an antidote to feeling anger and fear, and it is the fastest way to return to an expansive and open heart. The heart center, as we saw in the technique of "resting in the heart," is the gateway to the pure essence of awareness. An open, expanded heart center enables the pure essence of awareness to flow into the body-mind and into life itself. This is why a gratitude practice is transformative and can help clear the body-mind of the echoes of your former life.

Student: When can I experience abidance in the pure essence of awareness?

Master: This is not in your hands. There is no "Carter" in whose hands this achievement can be delivered. As you've experienced, awareness comes to a realization of itself in a body-mind. What appears as "practice" or "techniques" to cultivate abidance is only partially true... partially true from the vantage point of experiencing "Carter" again, so that such "Carter" can do something to help with the journey. This sense of "free will," which is what the choice of practicing appears to be, is only partially true. As you've seen, awareness alone *is*. Just like the Self-realization was no more than awareness coming to a recognition of itself, abidance is awareness experiencing abidance in awareness in this body-mind. It will happen when it will happen. The way to this abidance is abidance alone.

Student: [*pauses and closes eyes, then after a bit, opens eyes*] I see. This desire for abidance is the desire of "Carter." Wow! How quickly he snuck back in!

Master: [*smiles*] Yes, dear one. This is very tricky. The sense of a separate "I" is actually a force of nature itself. In awareness experiencing itself through and as a manifest world of separate beings and things, this sense of a separate "I" is a core force that makes duality arise from nonduality. In Indian traditions, this force is referred to as "Maya," the force of illusory creation. Until the body-mind is fully cleared of past echoes and impressions, the presence of those echoes and impressions are enough for this force, Maya, to reproduce the separate "I," "Carter" in this case. While "Carter's" former pursuits may be have been more material and mundane, now "Carter" is taking on the pursuit of becoming the self-realized master that you talked about. Now "Carter" wants abidance in the pure essence of awareness. And just like that, in a swift stroke and in an instant, "Carter" comes through the back door, to usurp the journey, so "Carter" has a reason to exist. It is part of the dream. It is part of the illusion that drives the existence and presence of a separate world in awareness.

Student: [*gasps and falls silent*] In a few quick moments, the experience went from the pure essence of awareness being aware of itself, to a clamoring to abide in it, driven by "Carter." Wow! This is so tricky and dangerous. It appears that I have to be vigilant of the arising of "Carter" all the time!

Master: [*smiles*] And who would like to be vigilant, may I ask?

Student: [*pauses and closes eyes, ponders, then opens eyes*] That is "Carter" again. Wow! Just like that I've fallen back in the trap!

Master: [*smiles*] Dear one. Close your eyes again. Take a deep breath. Relax. Listen to the sound of my voice. How do you know the sound of my voice?

Student: I am aware of the sound of your voice.

Master: And who or what is aware of being aware?

Student: Pure essence. Awareness. Awareness being aware of itself.

Master: And are you different from this pure essence?

Student: No. I am that. I am that pure essence.

Master: Dear one, open your eyes. See how much easier it was to revert to pure essence this time? And did that pure essence not exist always?

Student: Yes, Master. It always is. It alone is. And I am that.

Master: This oscillation between being pure essence and serving "Carter" may happen frequently or sometimes. Returning to being aware of being aware, returning to being that pure essence is all you can "do," and even that "doing" is not a doing of "Carter" but just another occurrence in awareness itself, in the process of awareness exploring its own nature through the apparent artifacts of a separate world, separate things, separate beings.

Student: I already feel this "oscillation" to be painful.

Master: Pain, dear one, is a pointer to truth. Notice the pain, and find who has the pain, and you will be back at the place of awareness being aware of itself. So don't feed the pain with resistance against it. Don't feed the pain by fighting with it. Don't ignore the pain. Simply follow it to its source...which is always awareness.

Student: I see it, Master. Awareness is the canvas upon which the motion picture of this world and its people and its things and its experiences are occurring. And it is awareness alone that is aware of the dream, the characters in it, and the experiences that occur, including the experience of Self-realization, the experience of waking up from the dream.

Master: That is right.

Student: So, in this body-mind, no matter what I do, no matter what I think, no matter what I experience in the world, no matter where I go, no matter where I turn, there is only awareness. And awareness alone is.

Master: Yes, dear one. This is what the Sufis say about this: "The face of God is upon everything."

Student: [*pauses and then starts crying*] Very humbling. Very, very, very humbling.

Master: As it should be. The deepest form of humility is the recognition that you, as a separate "I," do not exist. Awareness alone is.

Student: [*falls silent again and closes eyes, then opens eyes after a few minutes*]

Master: [*smiles*]

Student: Any attempt to use the mind, or the body, to think and do things pulls me away from the pure essence.

Master: [*silent, still smiling*]

Student: It seems like the only thing I could do is to not do anything and be truly quiet.

Master: And that—"Be silent"—is the advice given by the realized Master Sri Ramana Maharshi to his students, on the art of abidance in the pure essence of awareness. "Summa Iru," he would say in his native Tamil language, which essentially means, "Be quiet." More than being quiet by not speaking, he meant quiet in thoughts, resting in the heart center, as we discussed earlier.

Student: [*remains silent as minutes pass*]

Master: Yes, dear one, this is it.

Part 2 – Clarity

Having had the direct taste of being awake, the student has gone on to live life in the world and faces moments of clarity and also confusion. Over a few visits, he shares his thoughts and questions with the Master. What follows is a systematic dismantling of the grip of the mind on the direct experience of being awake.

To experience the clarity pointed to by the Master in this section, it may help if you first sit with the Exploration section, to slow down and get your own direct experience—that direct glimpse of Reality, that luminous awareness that is the essence of your being.

The Trouble With "I Know"

"Be silent. Silence is the gateway.
Where there is Silence, there is Freedom.
Where there is Silence, there is Peace.
Where there is Silence, there is Joy.
Where there is Silence, there is Love"
~ The Master

Student: Master, I am so grateful for your teachings. I came to you not knowing about nonduality or emptiness or enlightenment. Thanks to you, now I know!

Master: Nonduality is not nonduality. Nonduality alone is.

Emptiness is not emptiness. Emptiness alone is.

Enlightenment is not enlightenment. Enlightenment alone is.

"I know" shuts the door on knowing. Knowing is not mere knowledge, but that which is viscerally known in experience beyond words or concepts. "I know" is arrogance, the opposite of humility. Humility's deep meaning is "I don't know." Not knowing is the doorway to knowing.

"I know" has an "I" and a "know" and a "something" that is known. "I" is not real, and a separate-I is not real. What is left is "know" and "something" that is known. "Something" doesn't exist; it is not present in nonduality. What is left is "know." Without an "I" or "something," what is "know" or "knowing"?

Student: Thank you, Master. I needed that reminder on humility. It seems like I can often get caught up in thinking.

Master: Thinking of freedom, keeps you from Freedom.

Thinking of peace, keeps you from Peace.

Thinking of love, keeps you from Love.

Thinking of joy, keeps you from Joy.

Student: How then can I know Freedom, Peace, Love, and Joy?

Master: Be silent. Silence is the gateway.

Where there is Silence, there is Freedom.

Where there is Silence, there is Peace.

Where there is Silence, there is Joy.

Where there is Silence, there is Love.

Student: [*pauses*] Thinking is indeed the source of trouble. And it is such a habit.

The Importance of Direct Experience

"Truth cannot be known and pigeon-holed into concepts. Reality cannot be known through thoughts. However, Reality can be directly experienced. When the recognition of Truth occurs, the separate-I that you think you are is gone, and Truth alone remains, knowing itself. When the recognition of Truth occurs, the separate-I that you think you are is gone, and Truth alone remains, knowing itself."
~ The Master

Student: Master, I contemplated the insight you shared about Awareness, and I think I get it now.

Master: If you think you got it, if you think you know it now, then you most certainly don't know it. I use words like Awareness, Knowingness, and Love to point you to that which cannot be known through thought. The scriptures are quite clear about this.

Here's what the Tao Te Ching says:

"The Tao that can be named
Is not the Tao."

Here's what the Isha Upanishad says:

"It is not outer awareness,

It is not inner awareness,

Nor is it a suspension of awareness.

It is not knowing,

It is not unknowing,

Nor is it knowing itself.

It can neither be seen nor understood,

It cannot be given boundaries.

It is ineffable and beyond thought.

It is indefinable,

It is known only through becoming it."

Truth cannot be known and pigeonholed into concepts.

Reality cannot be known through thoughts. However, Reality can be directly experienced.

When the recognition of Truth occurs, the separate-I that you think you are is gone, and Truth alone remains, knowing itself.

Student: Not by thinking or doing can Truth be known. Another reminder to get out of my head.

Feeling Oneness

"How do you know of your mind, of your thoughts, of this "I" you think you are? What is it that is before the "mind" and is aware of the "mind" and its sense of being a "separate-I"? Find out. And the illusion of separation will shatter. One-ness will remain. And that is what you truly are!"
~ The Master

Student: Master, I look up at the sky at night and feel an awe. Yet, I can't honestly say that I feel One with the sky.

Master: What makes us different than the flowing rivers, the imposing mountains, the myriad animals, the birds in flight, the fish in the oceans, the green grass, the tall trees, the farmland, the grains, the fruits, the vegetables, this planet itself, the moon that whirls around it, the planets near us, the Sun around which they whirl, the galaxy of billions of stars through which they move and in which they exist, or the billions of galaxies in a virtually infinite unfolding universe?

Student: I feel different from it all.

Master: Yes. But from where does this feeling arise?

Student: From a belief that I am different from it all!

Master: Yes. From a mind that says that "I am not these. I am separate. I am distinct."

A mind that puts life in opposition to the Flow.

A mind that creates suffering.

A mind that veils the Truth of the Oneness of it all.

But what is this "mind" and this "I" that feels separate?

How are they even known? How do you know of your mind, of your thoughts, of this "I" you think you are?

What is it that is before the "mind" and is aware of the "mind" and its sense of being a "separate-I"?

Find out.

And the illusion of separation will shatter.

Oneness will remain.

And that is what you truly are!

Student: [*sighing*] The mind trap again!

Does God Exist?

"The simple aware existence that is God rises when the sense of being a separate-I falls. i.e. You are not God. In fact, the you, the "I" that you perceive yourself to be never really exists. God alone is."
~ The Master

Student: Master, does God exist?

Master: Existence is God.

Student: I exist. Am I God?

Master: "I am" is God.

Student: I don't understand.

Master: Sitting in silence, before any thought arises, are you aware of your existence? Try it and see now.

Student: [*pauses and becomes still*] Yes, there is a simple awareness.

Master: This simple awareness is what we express when we simply say "I am." This "I am" is an expression of existence, the fact that we are, that we exist.

Student: So are you saying that God is so close and is always present in the simple existence itself? I experience that as "I am." Can it be this simple?

Master: Yes. It is this simple.

Student: In the face of this understanding, before the thoughts, "I am tall," "I am twenty-four years old," "I am American," and so on, there is "I am," just the expression of existence itself. Existence that is God is so intimate. It has been present always. It's just overlooked by the "I am this" and "I am that" habit. Is this why hardly anyone recognizes or knows God?

Master: In a way of speaking, Yes. People seek God outside themselves. Even the spiritually adept can often seek God using their minds and come up with all sorts of ideas of what God may be! But there is something important you should carefully note. Go back to the silence, before thought arises, and be aware. Rest in that awareness. Go there now.

Student: [*pauses, becomes still and silent, and rests in the simple awareness before any thought arises ... and then opens eyes*]

Master: In the simple resting in that awareness, where was the "I," the person that you perceive yourself to be?

Student: That "I" that I normally perceive myself to be was absent.

Master: And yet, there was a simple awareness, right?

Student: Yes, Master. The "I" that I normally perceive myself to be was absent. Yet, there was a simple awareness.

Master: This is the key. The simple awareness that is God rises when the sense of being a "separate-I" falls. You are not God. In fact, the you, the "I" that you perceive yourself to be, never really exists. God alone is.

Student: [*in tears*] This must be what you've mentioned as the True Self. A simple existence, the "I am" that is not a separate entity, but the One alone.

Master: Yes. The Old Testament reveals this as the name of God: "I Am That I Am," a declaration of Existence itself. Ramana Maharshi referred to this as "I-I." A pointer to the only Self there is.

Many from One

"When you feel like you are separate from the One, and identify with a seemingly separate body-mind, you are already identified with duality. In this situation, for you, as that seemingly separate-I, the many seems to be truth. But in fact, there is only One."
~ The Master

Student: How did the One become many?

Master: The One never became many. The One is only One.

The idea of the One becoming many is an idea that is there only in duality! When you feel like you are separate from the One—and identify with a seemingly separate body and mind—you are already identifying with duality. In this situation, for you, as that seemingly separate "I," the many seems to be truth. But in fact, there is only One.

This is what Masters point to when they say, "You see the world not as it is, but as you are!"

This apparent illusion fades away on its own when you choose to rest in and as the True Self!

This is *not* a concept to believe in. This is a pointer to follow and know in direct experience.

Veiling

"When we are silent in body and mind, we can more clearly observe the rising and falling of thoughts. Something in us is aware of the rising and falling of thoughts, and that something isn't a thought. That which is aware of the rising and falling of thoughts is itself pure Awareness of True Self. When we simply observe the observing, we remain aware of being aware. This is freedom from thoughts and the veiling they create. This is abidance in True Self."
~ The Master

Student: Why am I often unaware? Why do I feel swept away by experiences that are occurring?

Master: Your thoughts effectively veil consciousness, the sense of being aware. This is why, very often, you are not aware of being aware.

Student: If that ever-present Awareness is my true nature, how can mere thoughts veil this?

Master: On a bright, sunny day, all it takes is one puffy cloud to obscure the Sun. And when that cloud covers the Sun from your vantage point, the Sun in all its brightness and glory is effectively veiled. The cloud, which can be readily dispersed by the blowing wind, can so easily veil the Sun. In this way, the thoughts that come and go, including that primal thought of "I am," which is presumed to be a "separate-I," veil the ever-present Awareness of True Self.

Student: Master, I understand now how thoughts, even as ephemeral and passing as they are, can veil the ever-present Awareness that is True Self. But why do I get stuck in the veiling of the thoughts?

Master: Thoughts have a sticky quality to them, especially that primal thought that you are a separate self, which is extremely sticky. This is why sages of the past have likened thinking and thoughts to a web woven by a spider.

Student: If thoughts have a sticky quality to them, how do I get unstuck from thoughts?

Master: When we are silent in body and mind, we can more clearly observe the rising and falling of thoughts. Something in us is aware of the rising and falling of thoughts, and that something isn't a thought. That which is aware of the rising and falling of thoughts is itself pure Awareness of the True Self. When we simply observe the observing, we remain aware of being aware. This is freedom from thoughts and the veiling they create. This is abidance in True Self.

Student: So the way to become unstuck from thoughts and thinking is to become aware of thoughts and thinking first?

Master: Yes.

Student: And that is why you've been telling us to cultivate a practice of meditation, anchoring in the breath! This enables me to not get stuck in and follow the train of thoughts by simply observing the thoughts rising and falling!

Master: Yes.

Student: This is so simple. Noticing the pure Awareness that is the True Self, and being aware of that Awareness, is actually so simple! And you're telling me that this is abidance in True Self, that this is the freedom I've been seeking! Why do I then feel like I'm chasing after something with my seeking, with my spiritual pursuits?

This is effortless, and yet I've been running up and down to different teachers, to different seminars, to exotic retreats, escaping to ashrams. . . Why all this drama?

Master: [*smiles compassionately*] Living unconsciously, being stuck in the veil of thoughts, as most people are, do you not experience the crazy drama of pursuing this or that? That very drama has come forth into your spiritual pursuit. When your frantic seeking ends, even if it is for awakening, you can see just how effortless it is to be yourself, to be your True Self.

Student: I am humbled, Master. What do you recommend for me?

Master: Be silent. Let the seeking go, let the striving go, let the thoughts and beliefs go, and simply be silent. Be aware of being aware. Be that awareness, and be free.

The Heart of Experience

"The heart of any experience is the knowing of it. Without the knowing of an experience, there is no experience at all."
~ The Master

Student: We talk of the essence, the heart of all things. Yet, for me, this is confusing, because I only see and experience different things in everyday living.

Master: Say you are seeing a flower. We can say that you are having an experience of seeing a flower. Can you have an experience of seeing a flower without knowing the experience of seeing a flower?

Student: [*pauses and thinks*] No!

Master: If I took away the knowing of the experience of seeing the flower, would there be anything left to that experience of seeing the flower?

Student: [*pauses*] Not really! No!

Master: We can say that the heart of the experience of seeing the flower was the *knowing* of the experience itself. Correct?

Student: Yes!

Master: The same is true, regardless of the specific experience. Whether you are seeing a mountain, a waterfall, a pet, a tree, a plate of food, or anything else, this is true—that the heart of the experience of seeing anything is the knowing of it. Correct?

Student: [*pauses*] Yes!

Master: The same is true, not just for the experience of sight, but also of hearing, smelling, touching, and tasting! Is that not so?

Student: [*pauses and thinks*] Yes! If I didn't know of a sight, sound, taste, smell, or touch experience, it doesn't exist for me.

Master: Indeed! The same is true for the experience of thinking too. If I didn't know of a thought, would there be anything there in that experience of thinking?

Student: [*pauses*] Yes!

Master: The same is true of body sensations and of recalling memories. Right?

Student: Yes!

Master: Effectively, what we are recognizing through this contemplation is that the heart of any experience is the knowing of it. Without the knowing of an experience, there is no experience at all.

Student: The heart of any experience is the knowing of it. How can I actualize this understanding in "everyday life"?

Master: In the midst of any experience, whether that is thinking, seeing, or tasting, you have the opportunity to go to the heart of it.

You can go from "having an experience" to the "knowing of that experience." And when you go to the "knowing," rest in the "knowing."

Initially when you do this, it may feel challenging. We are used to focusing on "things." And with some practice, we can do this focusing on "things." But what is suggested here is to go the other direction. Focus not on "things," but on that which knows "things." Go inside, so to speak. And this "knowing" is not an object, so "focus" on "knowing" is really not possible. Strive to do so, and the mind will soon fall into resting, because it cannot accomplish the job. But this is exactly what is needed: going from a "doing" task, given to the mind, to simply "being." This is a great step in moving from the unreal (changing experiences) to the Reality (knowledge) right in the midst of any experience.

Being that knowing that knows itself is true meditation.

Strive to go to the heart of any experience you are having, and experience the freedom from being bound in bewildering duality and the joy of being that which you are.

Helping Others

"As long as you continue to imagine that you are a separate being, separated from everything else, there is a continued imagination that there are "others". From the standpoint of Truth, there are no "others"."
~ The Master

Student: Master, how important is it to help others in my life?

Master: As long as you continue to imagine that you are a separate being, separated from everything else, you will continue to imagine "others." From the standpoint of Truth, there are no "others." Isn't that the very idea we express when we say that there is Oneness? Oneness isn't a situation where there is a you, and there are the other people, and you are connected as one. That is also a fantasy you have. In Truth, there is only One. Your essence, who you truly are, is that.

Student: But Master, I am still living in this fantasy as a separate person. That fantasy is the very basis of how I live in this world, so much so that all I perceive of myself and others is what feels *real* to me. What should I do?

Master: As long as this imagined falsehood continues to exist, by all means, do not judge others and bear anger, do not hold to worries and fear, be grateful for the gifts you have, be honest in everything you undertake, and be kind to yourself and others. This is a very meaningful practice to pursue as you continue your fantasy that you are a separate person.

Student: Master, will this practice help erase that fantasy?

Master: Yes. When you sincerely undertake this practice, it essentially thins out the ego, your sense of being a separate person. The deeper you go into it, the mind is more able to be still, the clinging withers, the more potential is there for a direct experience of clarity, a direct experience that you are not this fantasy of being a separate person that you are so wedded to now.

Student: Master, what happens when my imagination of being a separate person ends?

Master: Your sense that you are this body and this mind disappears, and with it the idea of "others" disappears too!

Student: When that occurs, how will I know that I'm not imagining it, like I imagine Oneness as being a connection between separate beings today?

Master: The sense of "I" will not exist, at least not in the form you are familiar with today. With the disappearance of that "I," the "separate-I," there is no mind that is separate to imagine anything. Your mind cannot comprehend this, as this occurrence implies the absence of the separate mind itself!

Student: Why is it important that I be rid of the fantasy of being a separate person?

Master: Today, as you are, is it true that you experience sadness just as much as happiness, stress that disturbs your peace, fears that arise to overwhelm you, judgments that make you behave in ways with other people that you are not proud of, guilt that eats you from within?

Student: Yes, Master. This is true. And it feels awful to see happiness arise only to disappear, peace to be felt only to vanish under waves of stress, fears come forth to crush everything, and guilt that is often unbearable.

Master: This is what the Masters call "suffering": the inability to simply rest in peace, love, or happiness. The inability to experience equanimity in the ebb and flow of life. You have the same experience of suffering as the character in your dreams, don't you?

Student: Yes, Master, I do.

Master: In your dreams, when your character has crazy up-and-down experiences, they come to an end when you wake up from the dream, yes?

Student: Yes, Master. When the dream ends, the crazy experiences in the dream are finished.

Master: The Masters say that your imagined existence as a separate person, and the up-and-down experiences you have as a separate person, is like a dream. The Masters simply and directly urge you to wake up from this dreamlike imagination so that you are no longer experiencing those ups and downs. That is real freedom—freedom from the sufferings that accompany your imagined existence as a separate person. What remains is the experience of the One, without a second. And that is not describable in concepts, so the Masters say to you that through pointers such as this: it feels like peace that is unbroken and love without its opposite.

Student: Master, there is a yearning for that freedom. But it feels so overwhelming to consider what it might take to be free like this.

Master: How much effort it is every night for you to wake up from your dreams?

Student: Master, I can't call that effort. It just happens.

Master: Go commit to the practice we talked about. The waking up will happen. When it does, it takes no effort either. And that is because you already are this eternal freedom.

Fresh Observation

"When the labeling [in the mind] stops, the one who labels disappears. What remains is that Silence, that alive Presence."
~ The Master

Student: Master, you tell me clearly to get out of my head and that thinking obscures Reality. Can you elaborate for me how to experience Reality without thought?

Master: [*holds a fresh carrot in his hand*] Take a look at this. What do you see?

Student: A carrot.

Master: Take away the label "carrot." What do you see?

Student: An orange root vegetable.

Master: Take away the labels "orange" and "root vegetable." What do you see?

Student: A conical thing.

Master: Take away the labels "conical" and "thing." What do you see?

Student: [*pauses and hesitates*] Something that bunnies eat.

Master: Take away the labels "something," "bunnies," "eat."

Student: [*dumbstruck*] I...I don't know.

Master: [*nods and says nothing*]

Student: [*gazing*]

Master: What are you thinking?

Student: There are no thoughts, Master. Just silence. Yet it is a silence that feels fully alive.

Master: [*smiles*] When the labels fall away, thoughts drop aside, and silence remains. And yes, that silence is fully alive. When you stopped labeling, what happened to the mind that was labeling? What happened to the one who was labeling?

Student: When I stopped labeling, there was only an intense living presence. Whatever was labeling inside me disappeared too.

Master: When the labeling stops, the one who labels disappears. What remains is that silence, that living presence. What are you feeling?

Student: Just that alert, living presence. And it feels strangely peaceful.

Master: That, dear one, is the experience of the True Self. That which is always aware, present, and at peace without its opposite.

Student: [*in tears*]

Master: [*smiles*] See, just right there in that simple carrot hid the presence, the awareness, the beauty, the peace of the True Self! All you had to do is see it with fresh eyes!

Student: [*closes eyes*]

Master: This is what the great artist Cézanne meant when he said, "The day is coming when a single carrot, freshly observed, will set off a revolution." Look at everything in the world around you with that same "fresh observation." The world cannot be the same any more for you.

Student: [*opens eyes and places hands together in prayerful reverence*]

Abiding in True Self

"Intensify your love for Self, the True Self.
That is what enables abidance in True Self."
~ The Master

Student: Master, how can I abide in the True Self?

Master: You love to walk in nature, don't you?

Student: Yes, Master, I do.

Master: Because you love to walk in nature, what do you do about it?

Student: Master, every evening, I take about an hour of time to get out of the home, and I walk in the beautiful park in my neighborhood.

Master: OK. You love to eat pizza, don't you?

Student: [*laughs*] Yes, Master, I do.

Master: Because you love to eat pizza, what do you do about it?

Student: Every so often in the week, when the opportunity arises to eat out, I like to go out and eat pizza or order pizza for delivery.

Master: OK. You have a three-year-old daughter. You really love her, don't you?

Student: [*smiles*] Yes, Master, I do. She is everything to me.

Master: Because you love your daughter, what do you do about it?

Student: Many things, Master. I've cut back on working twelve hours a day and try to get back home in the evening to be with her, to play with her. On the weekends, instead of being glued to the TV, I take as much time as possible to take her out to walk or play. I read books with her to just be with her. And so much more.

Master: OK. Because you love all this, you take the effort to do what it takes to engage in what you love. Is this right?

Student: Yes, Master. I do.

Master: And engagement in what you love actualizes what you love in your experience, does it not?

Student: Yes, it does, Master.

Master: The great awakened Master of our times, Ramana Maharshi, said this: "To abide in the Self, you must love the Self." So, how much do you love the Self, the True Self?

Student: [*pauses*]

Master: Yes, that's right. Most seekers miss this vital point. But it is OK. No need to be disappointed. It's always the right time to do the right thing. The great Master Adi Shankara said this: "Among the means and conditions necessary for liberation, devotion (*bhakthi*) alone is supreme. A constant contemplation of one's own Real Nature is devotion." What is devotion, really? Is it not the most intense form of love?

Student: [*in tears*] Yes, Master. Indeed.

Master: That is the way, dear one. Intensify your love for Self, the True Self. That is what enables abidance in True Self.

Part 3 – Pointers

Many who awake do not experience clearance of the impression of having operated as a separate person right away. Often, it takes time before one is able to abide in the wakefulness that is Reality, the True Self. In this interim period, there is an oscillation between Being and a self-identity on behalf of which experiences occur in the world of things. It is often bewildering to the person experiencing it. It makes them feel that they are doing something wrong. Or worse, they feel that the taste of Freedom they've been given is no longer accessible!

Since Truth cannot be taught as concepts, Enlightened Masters have always provided pointers to the Truth, to help students follow them to their own direct experience of the Truth over and over. These are not nuggets of wisdom for the mind. These are truly pointers meant for the student to follow to their own direct experience of what the Master is pointing to.

What follows are pointers from the Master to help the Student return to Being.

Suffering

Why are you agitated?

Getting angry, feeling worry,

Losing happiness

And peace?

Because somewhere inside

Something knows

This is wrong!

Something knows that

This is not your

Real nature!

Something knows that

You can't be

This little self!

The discomfort

The suffering

The limitation Are just signs

That this little self

And its experiences Are not real!

Something misses

The wholeness

The lasting peace The big love

The unwavering happiness

That is your

True Nature!

All your so-called

Normal, worldly experiences

Are pointing

To who you really are!

All your suffering

Is always pointing

To the Real You

That is Beyond suffering

Beyond birth

Beyond death

Beyond opposites!

The World

"For those who have obtained unobstructed knowledge of Self, the world is seen merely as a bondage causing imagination."
~ Ramana Maharshi

Conditioning and thoughts cast a world over what is.

The world as you experience it is entirely made from your own conditioning and thoughts.

The specific dualities that make up this world, for you, is a direct consequence of the unique distortions that exist due to your personal sense of being a "separate-I."

Let go of the "I" that holds the conditioning. Being alone remains. The "world" shines as Beauty.

Emptiness

"When I look beyond the mind, I see the witness. Beyond the witness, there is infinite intensity of emptiness and silence."
~ Nisargadatta Maharaj

The mind cannot understand emptiness. Emptiness is the complete absence of the mind and the fullness of Presence. Be silent. Let the mind's clinging go.

Liberation

"Peace of mind itself is liberation."
~ Ramana Maharshi

What we conventionally refer to as "Peace of mind" is actually a reflection of the "Peace" that is the True Self. Following the pointer of "Peace of Mind" to its source, "Peace" in the Heart is a return to Being.

Resting in and as Peace is pure Freedom. Resting in and as Peace is living awake!

The Unchanging

"What is bliss but your own being? You are not apart from being which is the same as bliss. you are now thinking that you are the mind or the body which are both changing and transient. but you are unchanging and eternal. that is what you should know."
~ Ramana Maharshi

Our thoughts come and go

Our feelings come and go

Our sense perceptions come and go

Our body sensations come and go

Our memories come and go

Our cravings come and go

Our attachments come and go

Our dreams come and go

But You don't come and go

   You are always present in all these experiences that come and go

   What is this You that doesn't come and go?

What is the unchanging element that stays on even as all these things come and go?

Find that which is unchanging in all these experiences

And you will find You, the real You!

Existence

Thoughts come and go
But you exist!

Days, months, years flow
You age with it all
But you exist!

In your experience
You have existed
Always!

Your existence
The one unchangeable element
Through Sukha and Dukkha[1]
And the coming and going
Of thoughts and beliefs and feelings!
What is existence

---

[1] Sukha = Happiness, Dukkha = Suffering (simplified translation from Sanskrit)

But a simple knowing
Of being?

And what knows
The knowing of the knowing
Of being?

The Pining to be Whole

"The wholeness we seek is our true nature,
who we really are."
~ Jack Kornfield

The rising anger

The fuming rage

Harsh judgment beneath

Is a pining to be whole!

The waves of worry

The pulsating stress

The grip of fear

Is a pining to be whole!

Desperate fluttering of a self

That wants to change the past

That wants to control the future

But can do neither!

Why does it want to do so?

The self itself is limitation

But inside, it misses Wholeness

Which is the Real True Self!

Anger and worry are reflections

Of the pining to be whole

From a self that can't be whole

Because Wholeness implies its death!

The Essence

"Only that which is always with you can be said to be yourself and if you look closely and simply at experience, only awareness is always 'with you'."
~ Rupert Spira

Is there anything to the world other than your experience of it?

Is your experience anything without the knowing of it? Is your experience anything other than the knowing of it?

Before the knowing of this or that, there is knowing alone. This is what is noticed and known as the active silence, the living gap between thoughts, the sacred pulsation of existence, the flow of what is.

In turn, your experience of anything is made of knowing and knowing alone.

And further, the world itself as you experience it is made of knowing and knowing alone.

From Knowing

Rises Mind

From Mind

Rises Body

From Body

Rises World!

When Body is still

And Mind is at rest

World disappears

Knowing alone shines

As the great bright light

That is Self!

I Am That I Am

"The essence of mind is only awareness or consciousness. When the ego, however, dominates it, it functions as the reasoning, thinking or sensing faculty. The cosmic mind, being not limited by the ego, has nothing separate from itself and is therefore only aware. That is what the Bible means by 'I am that I am'."

~ Ramana Maharshi

I Am That I Am

The Infinite. The Eternal

The Omnipresent. The Omnipotent.

The Omniscient Ocean of Awareness.

The wave rising from the Ocean

Becomes the experience

Of apparent duality, the world.

The world, as such

Is only made of the wave

And nothing more.

The wave falling to the Ocean

Becomes the experience
Of nonduality, True Self.

True Self alone is
The Ever-present Ocean
Of Awareness, Love, Bliss.

Seen from the lens of duality
Grace is the outward moving force
Causing the wave to rise from the Ocean
And the world-experience to form.
Seen from the lens of duality
Grace is the inward moving force
Causing the yearning for union
And the return to the Ocean.

The Ocean, the Sacred Presence alone is
Shining as the seeming "separate-I"
Shining as every world-experience
Reflecting to the I, its own true nature.

The Sacred Presence alone is

Ever-present as the Ocean of Awareness

As the timeless Bliss

As the endless Love.

So why is all this there?

It is the Divine Play, the Masters say

Of the Sacred Presence knowing Itself

As I Am That I Am

Love

"In ignorance, I am something; in understanding, I am nothing; in love, I am everything."
~ Rupert Spira

Love is Intimacy
Intimacy is no-separation
No-separation is Oneness
Oneness is Love!

Love is Listening
Listening is Being
Being is Knowing
Knowing is Love!

Love is Presence
Presence is Grace
Grace is Light
Light is Love!

Love is Wholeness
Wholeness is All
All is Peace
Peace is Love!

Love is Fulfillment

Fulfillment is Thankfulness

Thankfulness is Happiness

Happiness is Love!

Love is Existence

Existence is Awareness

Awareness is God

God is Love!

Surrender

"To remain in silence is surrender."
~ Sri V. Ganesan

Desire the experience of happiness, peace and love?

Whatever flows in the moment, you must allow!

Clamoring for the freedom vast as the sky?

Let go of everything that is about I, me, and my!

Want to be free from the fog of anger and fear?

Be the Great Light of Truth that is nearer than near!

Wish to be rid of the grip of confusing duality?

Be the Knowingness that is the only Reality!

What is this theme that recurs, you wonder?

This is the constant reminder of the need to surrender!

Belief vs. Faith

"Learn what surrender is. It is to merge in the source of the ego. It is enough that one surrenders oneself. Surrender is to give oneself up to the original cause of one's being."
~ Ramana Maharshi

Belief is a clinging

To a conceptual construct!

A tool to control

The shape of what is!

Faith is an acceptance

That we don't know!

A surrender, a leap

Into the abyss of what is!

Before Thought

"Silence is truth.
Silence is bliss.
Silence is peace.
And hence Silence is the Self."
~ Ramana Maharshi

What you are seeking

Through thought

Lies hidden

In plain sight

Before thought

As the Source

Of thought!

Being so,

How will you

Find it

Through thought?

You cannot!

But let thought

Fall back

Into silence,

Its Source

And you become

The One

You were seeking!

The Knowing Silence

Is it possible

That you fail

To notice True Self

Not because

It is distant

Or buried deep

But it is

Lying hidden

In plain sight?

Behind the mirage

Of the little self

And piercing

Into normal experience

It already rises

As happiness

As love

As peace!

Between one thought

And another

The Great Bright Light

That is the True Self

Rests shining

As knowing silence!

Yes to All

"Acceptance is not an activity of the mind."
~ Rupert Spira

Can you greet any rising experience with a Yes?

Regardless of whether it is judged by the mind as being good or bad, desirable or not, can you greet the rising experience with a Yes?

Saying Yes to all, in the moment, is radical acceptance of what is. In saying Yes to whatever rises in the moment, we are being love.

When we embrace radical acceptance of what is, personal preferences, attachments, desires, judgments — all of these are abandoned in favor of the simple "Yes" in the moment that greets the rising experience.

This is radical surrender too, where all things that are made of or driven by self-identity have been set aside, in favor of the simple "Yes" in the moment.

In turn, "Yes to All" is the mantra of radical freedom, where that which you are, simply shines![2]

---

[2] This idea of "Yes to All" is a radical acceptance of what is. The judging mind rises up to challenge this. "Yes to murder?" "Yes to abuse?" and so forth, it questions. The pointer here is not about a condonement of the content of the present experience the mind finds morally abhorrent! Any "pointer," as opposed to a mental concept, cannot be about the content of the mind, the beliefs of the mind, the judgments of the mind. Never! A real "pointer" is always to Reality. So in "practical terms," what is being suggested here? What has happened has happened? Do you find yourself arguing with what has happened? If so, that is resistance! Resistance is of the form, "This should not have happened," as if its goal is to change the past so that the present occurrence is not what it is! This is madness! Do you find yourself fuming in anger, judgment, resentment, or fear as a response to the interpretation of what has happened? If so, you are in your mind, toiling with the interpretation of what has happened. There is a better way. Notice what is happening—this is being aware of what is happening. Acceptance in its simplest form is the acknowledgment that what happened has happened. If you don't like the content of that happening, then act from your integrity about it in this moment. Say or do something now, as you see fit, about what occurred already. Or if you deeply experience the nature of Reality, you already know what is meant here by this pointer. The wise way for you is to return to Being.

114

Simply Being

"The ultimate truth is so simple; it is nothing more than being in one's natural, original state."
~ Ramana Maharshi

From being aware of this or that

To just being aware

To being aware of being aware

This is the pointer to

Simply Being That Which You Are!

Equanimity = Humility

"The power of humility, which bestows immortality, is the foremost among powers that are hard to attain. Since the only benefit of learning and other similar virtues is the attainment of humility, humility alone is the real ornament of the sages. It is the storehouse of all other virtues and is therefore extolled as the wealth of divine grace."
~ Ramana Maharshi

Accepting things as they are = Real humility

Being unswayed by this or that = Real equanimity

. . . one and the same!

What is common to both? Absence of the ego-self!

What is present in both? True Self!

The Master Key

"When your real, effortless, joyful grateful nature is realized, it will not be inconsistent with the ordinary activities of life."
~ Ramana Maharshi

Neither resistance

Nor clinging

Neither pushing

Nor pulling

Between asking

And receiving

Between conceiving

And doing

Lies gratitude

The Master Key

That beats back anger

That wipes out fear

That opens the heart wide

And moves Grace stronger

That lays foundation

To stand in Truth

That shines as love

And moves as compassion

The fast track

To entering the Flow

The direct path

To surrender

And rest in and as the Presence

The Infinite, Eternal One!

The Touch of Attention

"Grace is always present. You imagine it is something somewhere high in the sky, far away, and has to descend. It is really inside you, in your Heart, and the moment you effect subsidence or merger of the mind into its Source, grace rushes forth, sprouting as from a spring within you"
~ Ramana Maharshi

Grace is the creative force
Of the ever-present Source!
And where attention goes
Sacred Grace also flows!

Through the prism of body-mind
Flowing Grace you can find!
Body-mind prism distorts Grace
Creating Sukha and Dukkha in place!

Want no swings between Sukha
And the painful bouts of Dukkha?
Grace's flow should be pure
This is the only cure!

Pure Grace needs surrender

Rest attention in the heart of splendor!

"So be careful," the Masters mention

"Where you place your attention!"

The touch of attention

Is the kiss of Grace!

Attention moving through body-mind

Grace manifests Sukha & Dukkha!

Resting attention in the heart

Grace manifests unconditional love!

Zoom Out

You want to know
All about the truths
Of this world
That you live in
Why is all this here?
Why am I born?
What will happen when I die?
Does God exist?

But you are so
Zoomed into life
Seeing it through
A tiny pinhole
And you have lenses
With so many filters

Formed from the tangle
Of concepts and beliefs!

From this vantage point
You demand to know
All that needs to be known
About all that there is
But there is something limiting!

You are bringing a microscope
To a massive stargazing party
The wrong tool for the job!

Zoom out from the
Narrowband range of perceptions

Zoom out from the
Tangled mesh of concepts and beliefs

Zoom out further
To simply notice
The movement through perceptions
And the judgment through intellect
Zoom out further
To simply notice

The noticing itself
And rest in it!

Perception beyond perceptual organs
Disentanglement from the intellect
Freed from the confines of the body
A knowingness that knows itself!

A state of being
Where the little-I is gone
And the big-I that is
I Am That I Am remains!

No this or that
No pushing or pulling
No attaining or losing
Just simple being!
Zoom out
Again and again
Until what remains
Is You, the Real Essence!

The Real Alchemy

"See only that when you identify yourself with your personality you live in restriction. What is the use of the personality? Face your daily life free from restriction. See that all that is perceived, all that is thinkable is an expression of life, an extension of life. When you really understand that all existence is an expression of life and that the only mission of these expressions is to jubilate, to admire life, then you use your personality for thankfulness throughout your life; and then you use it in the right way."
~ Jean Klein

Start the day
With a thankful heart

Live the day
With a thankful heart

End the day
With a thankful heart

Each day

In this way

Witness the real alchemy

Whispered in secrets

Unfold from fantasy

Into reality!

Where judgment transforms

Into love

Where fear transmutes

Into peace

Where needing morphs

Into having

Where confusion mutates

Into clarity

Where doing transfigures

Into being!

Wisdom and Gratitude

"Wear gratitude like a cloak and it will feed every corner of your life."
~ Rumi

Wisdom is to value the things you have when you have them.

Gratitude is to be thankful for all that you have, for all experiences.

Gratitude is the highest form of wisdom.

The Overlooked Joy of Being

"Happiness is your nature.
It is not wrong to desire it.
What is wrong is seeking it
outside when it is inside."
~ Ramana Maharshi

In the open dance between asking and receiving

In the thankfulness that rises from both

Lies the pathway to the heart

And the overlooked joy of being!

Part 4 – Resources and Notes

Explorers of the innerscape, these keen observers of the human condition, these sages and Masters over the ages—across regions and traditions—have pointed to the same One Reality, the No-otherness.

This work is a flow based on the living example of these giants who have come and gone, as well as those who are among us today. What follows is a set of interesting resources and notes to aid your own abidance in your true nature!

Resources – Reality in One Verse

One source of inspiration from which the exploration above emerged is this ancient verse called Eka Sloki (literally "One Verse," but in the context it originated, should be more seen as "Reality in One Verse"). It is attributed[3] to the Enlightened Master, Adi Shankaracharya.

Master: By what light do you see?

Student: The sun by day, the lamp by night.

Master: By what light do you see these lights?

Student: The eye.

Master: By what light do you see the eye?

Student: The mind.

Master: By what light do you know the mind?

Student: My Self.

Master: You, then, are the Light of Lights.

Student: Yes, That I am.

There you have it...Truth and Reality in one single verse!

---

[3] http://greatmaster.info/ramanamaharshi/

Resources – Nonduality

Thousands of years ago, explorers of the innerscape found, through their direct experience, the foundations of Reality.

In India, this profound wisdom of Reality has been presented in the Upanishads (part of the Vedas), the Bhagavad Gita, and in later scriptural works like the Ashtavakra Gita, the Ribhu Gita, and more.

Existence, Reality is that which is, unchanging,
One without a second.

This is the essence of the wisdom, known as Advaita. Real Truth, our essential real nature, is this Reality.

"Advaita" literally means, "not two." "Advaita" translates into English as "nonduality."

Advaita, referred to as nonduality, gives rise to viewing it as a philosophy. But this is a very dry, intellectual, and limiting view of the totality of wisdom that the original tradition has to offer.

A more accurate translation of Advaita is *"No-otherness."* [4]

Advaita is not a philosophy. It is a live, vibrant, present experience of Reality, as Reality.

There are countless resources in the form of books and written works on this subject. And they are not contained just to the Indian Advaita tradition that I cite above, but they exist in Taoism, Buddhism, and many more offshoot Eastern traditions and even some Western traditions. The Tao Te Ching (particularly translations by Stephen Mitchell) is one such work, originating in ancient China, that shines with pointers to the Truth.

Since the advent of quantum physics, science has been led to many curious and paradoxical aspects of reality, and they parallel what the Masters of "nonduality" have experienced and shared. One interesting resource, if you are scientifically minded while being a spiritual seeker, is this one: "Science and Non-duality" (https://www.scienceandnonduality.com/about/nonduality/).

---

[4] Advaita is No-otherness. This gift of correct understanding came from Sri Nochur Venkataraman, through many of his talks. I have deep gratitude for him for this precious gift.

For me, what is more important than all these is the direct experience itself. The many teachings of "nonduality" point to the Truth, but if I am always enamored with the pointers and keep my attention on them, how can I experience the Truth? To experience the Truth, I need to let go of my attachment to the pointers and the teachings, and I need to let go the one who is attached. When I do, Truth is shining right there, always.

This work is meant to bring you that direct experience of "nondual" Truth, the No-otherness.

That said, if you are led to pursue the reading of some of the works on "nonduality," I'd suggest you look at the works cited above, and head over to the sites of the Great Masters and Contemporary Masters to navigate your journey.

Resources – The Great Masters

Many Great Masters in history have led countless humans from darkness to the light. Here are some Great Masters who have influenced my journey.

Sri Ramana Maharshi –

http://www.sriramanamaharshi.org/

All photos are public domain

"Happiness is your nature. It is not wrong to desire it. What is wrong is seeking it outside when it is inside."

~

"Reality is simply the loss of ego. Destroy the ego by seeking its identity. Because the ego is no entity, it will automatically vanish, and reality will shine forth by itself."

~

"... Bliss is not something to be got. On the other hand you are always Bliss. This desire [for Bliss] is born of the sense of incompleteness. To whom is this sense of incompleteness? Enquire. In deep sleep you were blissful. Now you are not so. What has interposed between that Bliss and this nonbliss? It is the ego. Seek its source, and find you are Bliss."

~

Nisargadatta Maharaj – http://www.nisargadatta.net/

Creative commons on Wikipedia

"All that a guru can tell you is: 'My dear Sir, you are quite mistaken about yourself. You are not the person you take yourself to be.'"

~

"The consciousness in you and the consciousness in me, apparently two, really one, seek unity, and that is love."

~

"Time is in the mind, space is in the mind. The law of cause and effect is also a way of thinking. In reality all is here and now, and all is one. Multiplicity and diversity are in the mind only."~

Papaji – http://www.avadhuta.com/

"If you address the mind with 'Who are you?' it will disappear."

~

"When the mind is quiet, all is Self."

~

"You are the unchangeable Awareness in which all activity takes place."

~

Annamalai Swami – http://realization.org/p/annamalai-swami/annamalai-swami.html

Photo courtesy David Godman

"If the thinker withholds his attention from rising thoughts or challenges them before they have a chance to develop, the thoughts will all die of starvation."

~

"You have to keep up the enquiry, 'To whom is this happening?' all the time. If you are having trouble, remind yourself, 'This is just happening on the surface of my mind. I am not this mind or the wandering

thoughts.' Then go back into enquiry 'Who am I?'. By doing this you will penetrate deeper and deeper and become detached from the mind."

~

"Bhagavan's [Bhagavan Ramana Maharshi's] famous instruction 'summa iru' [be still] is often misunderstood. It does not mean that you should be physically still; it means that you should always abide in the Self."

~

Resources – Contemporary Masters and Spiritual Teachers

For me, the Light for the journey to nowhere ("nowhere" → "now-here") was provided by many masters and teachers. Here are a few who have directly impacted my journey.

Frans Stiene – http://ihreiki.com/

Photo courtesy of Frans Stiene

My personal teacher, mentor, and friend, Frans Stiene, provided the scaffolding and framework through a very truthful and traditional understanding of Reiki ("Reiki" → "True Self") and has provided continual guidance toward recognition of Truth, that I am Reiki. If you are led to the notion of leading a life of deepening peace and happiness and wellness, healing yourself and others, with the continuous underpinning of awakening to your true nature, seek no further and reach out to Frans Stiene through his website above.

Rupert Spira – http://rupertspira.com/

Photo courtesy of Rupert Spira

Rupert Spira is that rare, genuine Light of Truth that shines so clearly in our present today. With years of learning and practice in the tradition of nonduality (Advaita, in ancient Indian tradition), Rupert woke up with his own teacher, Francis Lucille. Rupert Spira is a spiritual teacher who shares the Light freely through his website, videos, books, talks, and more. I have not been a formal student of Rupert's, but his very direct pointing at the Truth through Self-Inquiry and his works have been instrumental in the continual clarity that is emerging within this body-mind.

Mooji – http://mooji.org/

Creative commons on Wikipedia

Mooji is a spiritual teacher in the tradition of nonduality (Advaita). His teacher, Papaji, was a direct student of the Master Sri Ramana Maharshi. Mooji points directly to the Truth using Self-Inquiry, by enabling a person to follow their sense of "I" to its source. I have not been a formal student of Mooji's, but have experienced so much love and heartfulness flowing in his direct pointing, and this can be experienced by anyone through the many videos available online.

Ramanacharanatirtha Sri Nochur Venkataraman -

https://www.voiceofrishis.org/

More recently, I have found great inspiration and insights from the talks and Satsang with Sri Nochur Venkataraman, who I had a pleasure to listen to in person at Ramanashramam in Thiruvannamalai and in Chennai, India. There is absolute mastery in his talks that weave in scriptures, stories, and experiences—in multiple languages—while always having it all return to and anchor in the One Truth. Old mythological stories bear profound meaning in his talks. Ordinary experiences connect to the sacred in his eloquent and engaging discourses. Duality melts away, revealing the Nondual Truth in the silence from which his words arise. The One Truth is No-otherness.

Peter Cutler - https://n-lightenment.com/

Photo courtesy of Peter Cutler

Peter Cutler is an author, monk, and spiritual teacher based in Sedona, Arizona, whose nondual pointers have been a great source of welcome clarity on the journey. Peter's many daily posts point to abidance in What Is.

Guthema Roba - https://www.facebook.com/gbroba

Photo courtesy of Guthema Roba

Truth cannot be expressed in concepts or words. Masters only point to the Truth, and it is up to us to follow the pointer to our direct experience. That said, Guthema Roba is a mystic poet, in whom Truth gushes in words through his poems, like I've rarely seen anywhere. They are a daily staple of the celestial nectar of immortality for me!

Many other teachers, authors, and speakers have been invaluable at various junctures in the inner journey for me. Here are a few: Adyashanti, Byron Katie, David Godman, Deepak Chopra, Eckhart Tolle, Eknath Eswaran, Fred Davis, Hyakuten Inamoto, Jeddah Mali, Jon Kabat Zinn, Gangaji, Krishna Das, Martha Beck, Mike Dooley, Paul Brunton, Pema Chodron, Ram Das, Sri Sri Ravi Shankar, Sri V. Ganesan, Stephen Mitchell, Susan Verghis, Swami Kriyananda, Swami Rama, Swami Sarvapriyananda, Swami Tadatmananda, Swami Vivekananda, Swami Yogananda, Thich Nhat Hanh, Wayne Dyer, Wayne Wirs, and William Rand.

Resources – Self-Inquiry

The experiential exploration presented here is based on the teaching of Sri Ramana Maharshi, called Self-Inquiry (also known as Self-Enquiry).

Progressive paths to Self-realization tend to have an individual as the practitioner, firmly rooted in their self-identity as a distinctly separate person, a separate-I on whose behalf a lifetime of practice is undertaken, learnings achieved, self-improvement made, and ego thinned out over time. They are individuals who, at some future date, will obtain the highest achievement of Self-realization, accompanied perhaps by spiritual fireworks, celestial experiences, and cosmic bliss. While this journey is representative of the vast majority of practitioners, the expected conclusion of great enlightenment simply does not occur, except in the rare, few Masters. This is factual reality.

Sri Ramana Maharshi, who himself had his awakening as a young boy, said that while all spiritual paths could take a practitioner to that end goal of Self-realization—and that each person can pursue the path they feel inclined and ready to undertake—also said the direct path to knowing one's true nature is Self-Inquiry.

All thoughts arising in your body-mind always do on behalf of the separate-I that you think you are. Who is this I? Follow the I-thought to its source, Sri Ramana Maharshi said, and the Truth will be revealed about the true nature of this I.

This work can be thought of as a guided form of Inquiry, an experiential exploration of the true nature of reality—a journey, as it were, to the source of the "I," to recognize the true nature of that "I."

Self-Inquiry is an experiential and direct pointing to the nondual Truth. Practitioners who diligently apply Self-Inquiry can come to an experiential recognition of their True Nature. But does this recognition necessarily mean that the practitioner is totally free from the grip of illusion, the grip of the identity of being a separate-I? Only rarely does experiential recognition of True Nature, what is known as enlightenment, mean total freedom from illusion. In most cases, the real practice begins, by abiding in and as the True Nature, through Self-Inquiry.

In this sense, the experiential application of Self-Inquiry separates enlightenment, the recognition of one's True Nature, from abidance in and as the True Self. Self-Inquiry doesn't necessarily get rid of the practice as a practitioner. But what it does is dispel the illusions around being a separate person, with a separate identity, and leave the practice of the remainder of the life of the body-mind to one of simply abiding as the Truth that has been experientially known.

The works of the Great Masters and the Contemporary Master and Teachers cited earlier can be of great help in abiding in and the True Self that you already are. Specifically, Rupert Spira talks to the modern practitioner in such a simple and clear language that he has made Self-Inquiry very approachable for people of this era.

Resources – Other Methods

Is Self-Inquiry the only path to Self-realization? No! There are many paths to Self-realization, as outlined below. Self-Inquiry is seen as a direct path because it follows a simple path of exploration to the experiential knowing of the Self here and now.

Yoga itself is a term that means union (union with the Divine). The ancient Indian scripture the Bhagavad Gita outlines three paths of yoga, though many masters espouse four paths (http://www.sivananda.org/teachings/fourpaths.html). A person may choose any of these paths that resonate with their own traits and personality and arrive at the same goal: union with the Divine.

- Path of Action: Karma Yoga

- Path of Devotion: Bhakti Yoga

- Path of Knowledge: Jnana Yoga (aka Gyana Yoga)

- The Royal Path: Raja Yoga

Karma Yoga is the path of selfless action. People who are work and action oriented will find this a suitable path for them. The central idea is "selfless work," i.e. work done without thought for personal gain or reward. This approach builds a steady detachment to the outcomes from work and in turn tames the separate ego-self.

Bhakti Yoga is the path of surrendering oneself to God through unconditional love for God. People who are able to feel strong emotions and who are moved more readily by deep experiences will find this a suitable path for them. Chanting or singing praises of God are key ways a person is able to transmute their own emotions into pure love for God. This unconditional love for God implicitly wears out the separate ego-self.

Jnana Yoga is the path of wisdom. The central idea is to use the mind to inquire into its own nature. Self-Inquiry, as I discussed earlier, is a key method in the wisdom path to awaken to the experiential recognition of one's true nature. Jnana Yoga, as practiced through Self-Inquiry, is a relatively simple and direct method to know the True Self from experience. However, without some prior practice that has built some degree of selflessness creating the ability to focus the mind, this path can be a trap resulting in the mind speculating about itself endlessly.

Raja Yoga is seen as the royal path by many masters. It provides a comprehensive framework of precepts, postures, breath-control techniques, mind and body control techniques, as well as meditation techniques. Meditation is a central part of this path. Its holistic approach that engages body and mind in different dynamic ways may be attractive to many people.

The examples above are from the spiritual traditions of India. Similar examples abound in Buddhist traditions, Sufi traditions, Taoist traditions, and others. People who are kinesthetically tuned may love the physical movements of Taoist methods, Yoga, and others. People who are aurally tuned may love the chanting and toning methods of many traditions. People who are visually oriented might find it more appealing to follow visually guided meditations as their preferred technique.

The traditional system of Reiki offers a set of tools, which include meditations, chanting, hands-on-healing, precepts to live by, and initiations or spiritual blessings.

When practiced consistently and diligently, these tools systematically erode the grip of the ego-self in our lives. As the ego-self falls aside, the power of True Self, which is always here and now, is unleashed into the present experience. Calmness rises. Compassion grows. Gratitude expands. Peace is palpable. And one is able to be truly Present in any situation with any person. It is in these circumstances that sheer miracles unfold effortlessly.

Any of these paths are reasonable practices to get going on the inward journey. What is most important? Your consistent practice with your preferred methods! The clarity that comes from working with a real, genuine teacher can be an immense blessing.

A caveat for the seasoned practitioner: we often see practitioners investing twenty years, thirty years, or even more on one of these paths and getting frustrated that they are not breaking free, that they are not achieving the goal of union with the Divine, that Self-realization! The trap of progressive paths like these can be that the practice is taken on by a separate self, which incrementally wants to improve itself to the point that it can know the True Self while still being a viable entity as a separate self. At some point, you have to let go of that self-image, that self-identity you've been serving, that separate self that has been trying to enlighten. You simply have to let it go. Why? That which you are seeking is what is seeing. The True Self you seek is already here, and it is in that Awareness of the True Self that any experience you call your own is even occurring. How many mountains will you climb? How many forests will you go into? How many retreats will you take with different teachers? How long will you go on doing things to achieve your goal of union, of Self-realization? At some point, you have to let go of the ego-self, and there and then the light of True Self shall be known in experience.

You, the separate you, cannot enlighten. That is simply impossible. When the separate-you is set aside, the light you've been seeking can simply be experienced.

Glossary

Abidance – a continuous experiencing of Reality, as it is. Real enlightenment is Abidance. It is also complete freedom.

Advaita – (*Sanskrit*) not two. This is a pointer to Reality. Often translated into English as "non-duality", Advaita is better understood as No-otherness.

Ananda – (*Sanskrit*) bliss. Bliss evokes some exotic mental state or some sort of peak experience. In reality, Ananda is better understood as Peace-Love-Happiness without their opposites.

Awakened Master – a human who has awakened to their true nature as Reality.

Awakening – the experiential glimpse of one's true nature, Reality.

Awareness – true nature, Reality, cannot be described in words or concepts, because it is before the mind. Reality can be directly experienced. For communicating the nature of Reality, Masters invoke some key attributes. One of them is pristine or pure Awareness. Awareness is the raw knowingness that is devoid of objects. Awareness is what is, unchanging, before awareness of this, or awareness of that arises in experience.

Beauty – the experience of pure love in form. The world as it is, is Beauty, because, in Reality, it is just Love, masquerading.

Being – what is prior to mind. Before thought, feelings, memories, expectations, attachments, resistance, clinging, perceptions, feeling, sensations and such, lies the stateless state that Existence as-it-is. Being is Reality.

Bhakti – (*Sanskrit*) the art, practice and experience of devotional surrender to the Divine.

Bliss – normally seen as a state of ecstasy, a heightened state of mind, Bliss is better seen as a steady Peace-Love-Happiness without their opposites.

Chit – (*Sanskrit*) Awareness. The unchanging essence through which awareness of ourselves and the world is possible. Can also be seen as Knowingness, in its pristine form, before knowing of this, or knowing of that arises.

Divine – God, Higher Power, Source, Tao, Brahman. Named as such in many ways, the names should not be confused for what it really is. What it really is, is Reality, One without a second, unchanging, as it is.

Duality – the human experience of opposites – cold-hot; up-down; good-bad. Every human experience is riddled with opposites. No human experience can rest in just one aspect. If one is happy now, it is not too long before, that its opposite, unhappiness shows up in one form or another.

Dukkha – (*Sanskrit*) Suffering. Any experience that comes in opposition to peace-love-happiness.

Ego-self – the sense of personal identity that is caused by the sense of otherness, the sense of being separate from the wholeness that is life, that is the world. Not to be confused with the "ego" as defined in modern Psychology (the id, the ego, and the super-ego).

Emptiness – normally seen as devoid of any thing, this heavily misunderstood term originating in Buddhism (*shunya* in *Sanskrit*) is better seen as the experience present when one is empty of their ego-self.

Enlightenment – being the Light. An experience of one's true nature, which is beyond the coming and going nature of experiences of one's ego-self and the world it presumes to experience. An experience that feels like Peace-Love-Happiness without their opposites. And experience that feels like Freedom from the limitations of ego-self. Real Enlightenment, or Abiding Enlightenment is the continuous experience of Reality, the One without a second, unchanging as it is.

Flow – the mysterious state in which doing happens effortlessly. A state of harmony with what is, in which non-doing results in all the doing needed, in perfection.

Freedom – the unbroken experience of Wholeness, of Reality as it is.

God – see *Divine*.

Grace – the apparent emanation from, and movement of Presence. The creative force behind all of creation, that precipitates into apparent form, the boundless formless.

Great Bright Light – (*dai komyo* in Japanese, and in the system of Reiki) the Light of Pristine Awareness, i.e. Reality, True Self.

Happiness – the unchanging Reality, one's real nature. Not to be confused with the *happiness* that comes and goes in the experience of oneself as a separate person. Real Happiness is what already is, and shines always in the Heart.

Heart – the core of it all. Not to be confused with the physical heart, or the energetic heart (i.e. heart center). Though unfailingly, when one rests attention in the heart center, one gets to the Heart, True Self.

Holy Spirit – a term from the Christian theology of the Trinity (Father, Son, and Holy Spirit).

Jnana – (*Sanskrit*) Wisdom without its opposite. Real Clarity. Emerges from Heart.

Knowingness – see *Awareness.*

Liberation – the experience of Real Freedom. Being free of the grip of ego-self. Abidance in True Self. Also known in *Sanskrit* as Nirvana, as in the state of the Buddha's steady Enlightenment.

Light – the pristine Awareness, through which anything is known. Also see *Great Bright Light.*

Love – the inseparable Wholeness, the eternally intimate Source, True Self. Not to be confused with love, in human experience, which has a very coming and going nature to it, here now, gone later. Real Love is unchanging, Reality, as it is.

Master – refers to a person in a steady state of Enlightenment, in Abidance.

Maya – (*Sanskrit*) the mysterious force of illusion that seems to create a multifarious world, where Reality, One alone without a second, exists. Maya is what produces duality from non-duality. Maya is what seems to birth otherness when No-otherness alone is.

Mind – the process of one thought after another, with its secondary artifacts of fructification of thoughts into beliefs, memory and more.

No-otherness – Reality. The absence of otherness. What is, as it is, unchanging, One without a second. This is the real meaning of the *Sanskrit* word Advaita, which has been casually translated as nonduality. Your real nature.

Non-duality / nonduality – originally from *Sanskrit* Advaita. See No-otherness.

Peace – the unperturbed serenity, the eternal Silence, that is Heart. Not to be confused with peace, in human experience, that comes and goes, and is easily lost to anger, worry, fears and more. Peace is your real nature.

Presence – the direct experience of Being. Existence, as it is, unchanging, is Presence. The source of Grace.

Quantum field – the substratum of material reality, according to Science, is this ever-present, fluxing field of energy, which is what gives rise to matter.

Reality – what is, as it is, unchanging, One without a second. Not to be confused with reality, in human experience, which is more often than not, an artifact of one's mind. We don't see the world as it is, but as we are.

Sat – (*Sanskrit*) Truth. Pristine Awareness, devoid of awareness of this or that. Reality. True Self.

Self-realization – the experiential recognition of one's true nature, as Reality. The experiential recognition of the absence of ego-self.

Self-inquiry – the process of inquiring into one's real nature, through a question like "Who am I?" An ancient method in the Path of Wisdom (in *Sanskrit, Jnana*

Yoga), very simply elucidated for the modern world, by the great awakened sage, Sri Ramana Maharshi.

Separate-self – see ego-self.

Sukha – happiness experienced in human form, which comes and goes, and has no steadiness to it. This happiness, in the world, is mistaken to arise from possessing or experiencing things and people and so forth, when in fact, its real source is the Happiness that is within, the Happiness that is Heart, Reality. *Sukha* in human experience is the dual opposite of *dukkha*.

Upanishad – (*Sanskrit*) to sit near. Ancient Sanskrit scripture that captures Truth revealed to Masters in direct experience, and learned by students sitting near a Master. Part of the Vedas, and seen as the essence of the Vedas, for its direct pointers to Truth.

Vedas – (*Sanskrit*) knowledge. Ancient Sanskrit scriptures from India that is the total embodiment of knowledge from the practical ways of life through rituals and hymns, to precepts and philosophy to guide life, to preparatory practices to undertake the inner journey, to wisdom explorations to realize one's true nature, i.e. Self-realization, and pointers to living awake.

Tao Te Ching – ancient Chinese scripture, attributed to Laotse (aka Lao Tzu), which is the core text of Taoism (aka Daoism). It talks of the way of the flow.

True Self / Self – one's real nature. The One without a second, as it is, unchanging. Reality. Truth. Infinite. Eternal. Sat. Chit. Ananda.

Truth – see Reality.

Union – the mystical reconnection between one who's seen themselves as separate with their Source, the Divine. Commonly used idea in *Bhakti* traditions, where the person feeling separate, misses the Divine like a lover missing their beloved. The Divine is referred to often, in these traditions, as the Beloved. The quest of the spiritual path is the Union with the Beloved. The utter dissolution of the personal-self / ego-self with the One, without a second.

Wholeness – what is, as is, from which nothing is excluded, and to which nothing can be added. Reality. Truth. True Self.

About the Author

Name: Sundar Kadayam

Place of birth: India

Place of residence: USA

Work: Technology entrepreneur (https://www.linkedin.com/in/sundarkadayam), healer, writer, teacher.

Practice: Self-Inquiry, the direct path to Self-Abidance, Bhakti (devotional surrender), and Traditional Reiki (as a path to Self-realization and abidance in and as True Self).

Blog: http://NoOtherness.com/

Articles: On http://IHReiki.com/, my teacher Frans Stiene's website, search for <Sundar Kadayam> for articles on Reiki and the spiritual path

Email: skadayam@presevo.com

About the No-otherness Series

This work, Awaken, is the first of a series of offerings on No-otherness. It is an aid to enable experiential glimpses into the wakefulness of one's real nature.

At the time of this writing, two more follow on works are contemplated.

Arise: Learn to Live Awake would introduce one to the art of living awake through real world stories and practical tips. This is an aid to stabilize the glimpses of wakefulness into a way of wakeful living.

Abide: Pointers to Living Awake would present poems and select writings to help one who is committed to living awake, be free of the receding echoes of self-identity and return to their real nature, No-otherness, over and over easily. This is an aid to abiding as Reality, living in the world but not of it.

Gratitude

To Andrea Conway for being a coach and accountability partner at important junctures in life. To Sue MacDonald writer and editor extraordinaire, for always lending a hand to improve my writing. To Zeynep Yilmaz, who has been a fellow traveler on this journey since 2014. To Maria Kammerer, who is always ready to help and whose own journey is an inspiration to me and others...a heartfelt thank you.

To my father, K. V. Ramachandran, whose incredible sacrifices provided a platform for our family, and whose final sacrifice for three of his final years in deep bedridden suffering kicked off this incredible journey for me to here and now. This was his final blessing for me, one that is meant to keep on giving to the world.

To my paternal grandfather, K. R. Venkatram, who I grew up with, and to my aunt and grandma in Chennai, India, deep gratitude for sowing the seeds of the Mystery in my heart through stories of Hanuman, the hero of the epic Ramayana, and instilling practices whose profound value I only came to understand during this journey.

To my life partner and friend, Uma, who has stuck with me for over three decades, through my evolving quirks and idiosyncrasies, through the incredibly challenging journey on the spiritual path, and for so many things I cannot put in words. For your constant presence with me, and the space it provides for my exploration, my heart opens wide in gratitude.

To my Mom, in her mid-80s at the time of this writing, who has been a willing and open student of mine for over fifteen years, who has learned the healing art from me and helps others routinely with healing, and who has sincerely tried to change her crusted ways of thinking and living to favor and savor peace. You've said often to me, with a great sense of pride, that your son is bringing to you, the senior one in the family, profound and practical wisdom, like Lord Muruga brought to his Father, Lord Shiva. Humbled as I always am to hear this kind of admiration, what is most important to me is that you've been a source of inspiration to teach and share with others the blessings that move through me in abundance.

To my maternal uncle, Sri N. Ramgopal, whose life of devotion to the One in many forms, has been a great inspiration. He also helped kick off my spiritual journey after my dad was in coma, with a short pilgrimage, that opened the door to a life of miracles. Deep gratitude for his blessings.

To family and friends, who simultaneously witness the journey with awe and incredulity, with excitement and more than just a bit of disbelief, and yet provide the freedom to do what is needed, and just permit me to be...to you all, gratitude. To those of you who deserved to be singled out and named here, but which I may have failed to do, know that my heart is full of gratitude for you all.

To the people who, while living, were an inspiration, and whose passing drove the determination to awaken and remain awake. My schoolmate and childhood friend, V. N. Swaminathan, who taught me to not be so serious about life, and retained his amazing sense of humor even as he undertook the journey to awaken. My brother-in-law, M. R. Sivaraman, who kindled my own passion, through his passion for learning and keenness to understand any topic in life, and who in passing, left me an amazing spiritual gift. There's my aunt Mrs Subbalakshmi who poured her love into me and took care of me in my growing up years. My paternal uncle Dr. K. V. Gopalakrishnan, in whose home and presence I was moved to feel the power of devotion to Hanuman. My maternal grandfather Sri Narayanan instilled in me the passion for healing, through his own pursuit of homeopathy. My father-in-law Mr G. Ganesan, who loved and supported me as if I was his own son, and stood by me through the times when profound life questions arose. There are so many others, friends and family members alike, whose lives, likewise, touched me in ways to nudge me onto the right path in my journey. To all of them, my heartfelt gratitude.

To the many early reviewers and their feedback to improve this work, to you all, my deep gratitude.

To the group of amazing people in the greater Cincinnati region, who are sincere seekers and practitioners, the regular opportunity to share space and practice with you at "Peace House" has been and continues to be invaluable... to you all, gratitude.

To Joshua Lisec. Gratitude for his help with the professional editing, publishing preparation, and more. It was such a relief to have a professional take over all those aspects from me. Joshua's diligence, timely, high quality work, and flexibility have made the transformation of this work into a print publication easy.

To the Great Masters and the Contemporary Masters and Spiritual Teachers, whose works and teachings have enabled the recognition of Truth, and the flow of the same... heartfelt gratitude.

To life itself, who stands ready to whisper her secrets anywhere and anytime, asking nothing of me or from me except a simple, open, nonjudgmental, unhurried presence...deep gratitude. The one whispering her secrets, the one listening sans judgment, the canvas of awareness upon which this and all occurs, these are intimately inseparable, just One.

Who then writes this? And who reads this?

Who is Master? And who is student?

Who is teaching? And who is knowing?

What is being asleep? And what is being awake?

What is wisdom? And what is ignorance?

What is Reality? And what is illusion?

Love Alone Is.

And You Are That!

The Path Forward

Awakening to our True Self is the destiny for all humans. In fact, the very purpose of human life is to awaken to our Real Nature!

The direct experience of Reality affects each person differently. Few are those people who experience awakening that remain entirely awake from that initial experience. It is far more common for it to take a fair bit of time for the experience of awakening to stabilize in the body-mind, which has lived on behalf of a separate self-identity. It is entirely common that people who taste awakening experience an oscillation between moments of being awake and swaths of time in which the body-mind returns to the control of the seeming self-identity, this separate-I.

For me, the oscillation has been heavy and strong and has lasted years. It was a source of great consternation as it was occurring. In the midst of this strong oscillation, I felt far too often that what the Masters experienced, as an Abidance in True Self, that was going to be denied to me. I felt like some of these

169

Masters were fortunate and lived at a time where they could go off into the forest, or up into the mountains, or withdraw themselves into caves, renouncing normal worldly life, but I couldn't, living in this world as a householder, an entrepreneur, with worldly responsibilities. I felt doomed to struggle through this!

It turned out this was all more mistaken stuff from a mind running amuck under the control of a seemingly separate person!

Just like a pendulum that has been set in motion will keep swinging from one side to another until it comes to rest in the middle, this oscillation too will come to an end. This logical observation is super empowering.

Why does this oscillation occur?

Simple! The belief in a separate identity is still there in some measure. That is why periods of time elapse in which the experiences appear to be occurring on behalf of that self-identity. At some time, this belief in separateness dissolves entirely. When the final shards of the belief in separation fall, there is a palpable freedom. Whatever is happening is seen as just happening, not as happening to "me"! And this deepens in ways that cannot be described in words.

In the meantime, what can one do, when experiencing oscillation?

Simple! When you notice the experience in the moment, to have a constricting, limited, confused, or perturbed quality, that experience is under the control of the "I" that you thought you were. You can immediately apply Self-Inquiry in that moment to verify if the "I" that was seen to not exist in the initial awakening experience, somehow has come back alive. My own experience is that this simple practice always revealed the same nonexistence of a separate self, which in turn was accompanied by resting in Being. And over time, the final shards of the belief in a separate self just fell. Experiences of seeming separateness was simply seen as happenings happening. Nothing personal is going on here. Nothing personal was ever going on. Nothing personal will ever happen. And with that realization, there is more and more freedom that comes into the experience in the moment. In time, this constant returning to Being True Self establishes the foundation for Abidance in True Self!

During the period of oscillation, I've found that the direct pointers of the Masters always helped with returning to Being. The key thing to remember with the Masters' pointers is that they are not knowledge nuggets for "you" to accumulate. They are pointers, and as such you have to walk from the pointer to what is being pointed at.

Abidance in and as True Self naturally takes root. And this is entirely logical, because, after all, the True Self alone is!

To summarize the experience of awakening, we can consider it in these terms:

- Initially, there is an **unaware living**, where the sense of "I" has never been questioned, and inherently limited life experiences of a world tumble into being, in bewildering duality!

- Then comes the great blessing to **Awaken**, which shows, in direct experience, the True Self that we are and also shows that the separate-I never existed!

- With the glimpses of awakening in direct experience comes the possibility to **Arise** from dreamful living and learning to live awake!

- This is followed by the profound opportunity to live awake, to **Abide** in and as the True Self!

Again, please do not mistake this to be some sort of three-stage process or any other conceptual matter! It is not. The True Self alone is. Whether we know it or not, the True Self alone is *always unchanging*. What is described here is a halfway pointer to what the experience of awakening is like, just to give some affirmation to the person who has experienced awakening and now desires to live awake. Please note that this is only a halfway correct pointer, because a "you" cannot "live awake"! The One Reality alone is! To say "Abidance," to say "live awake"—these are halfway pointers spoken to one firmly rooted in a separate identity. From the vantage point of Awareness, the True Self, if one can even speak like that, there is One No-otherness!

Look to pointers from the Masters, some of whom we cited earlier, and follow those pointers to return to the direct experience of Being. Do so over and over. Choose to return to Being whenever you notice that your experience is feeling personal. In its own time, the oscillation will come to an end, as the True Self remains fully rooted as itself in the body-mind experience. After all, self-identity, body, mind, experiences, the world—all this is just Love masquerading!

The Grace that brought you the glimpses of awakening will also bring the fruit of abiding wakefulness, the continuous experiencing of Being, and the consistent unfolding of living awake as True Self.

An Invitation to Embrace your Destiny

Like a seed in soil

Germinating in the warmth

Fed by water

Nourished by sunlight

So also, dear One

The womb of creation

Awaits your blossoming

Crack open from your shell

Root in life's flow

Grow toward the light

Reach for the skies

Embrace life's riches

And share it forward

Through fragrant presence

Through loving words

Through kind actions

You are not here

To lead a limited life

Confined by the prisons

Of your beliefs
You are not here
To struggle and suffer
And eke out
A meager living

What brings forth
Millions of life forms
And provides for
Their abundant growth
Also brought forth
The precious form
That you are
And gave you
An awareness of yourself
So that you may
Begin to know
Of the kingdom of riches
That is your real home
And be free of
The bonds of ignorance
Embracing your
Real destiny of Union

Made in the USA
Monee, IL
05 February 2020

21299546R00113